Pursuing Sanctification

How To Receive Your Real Inheritance From God

Elect Lady Vanessa Johnson

Foreword By Apostle Garfield Curlin

A Ready Writer's Ink Publishing

Brookfield, Wisconsin

Pursuing Sanctification
How to Receive Your Real Inheritance from God
By Vanessa Johnson

 A Ready Writer's Ink Publishing
Post Office Box 2287
Brookfield, WI 53008
http://www.areadywritersink.com

© 2010 Vanessa Johnson. All rights reserved. No part of this book may be reproduced, scanned, or distributed in any printed or electronic form without permission. Please do not participate or encourage piracy of copyrighted materials, which are in violation of the author's rights. Purchase only authorized editions.

Unless otherwise indicated, Scripture quotations are taken from the King James Version of the Holy Bible.

Scripture quotations taken from the Amplified Bible, copyright © 1954, 1958, 1962, 1964, 1965, 1987 by The Lockman Foundation. Used by permission. www.Lockman.org

Scripture quotations taken from the Maxwell Leadership Bible, copyright © 2002, by Maxwell Motivations, Inc.

Scripture quotations taken from The Holy Bible, New King James Version, copyright © 1982, by Thomas Nelson, Inc.

Scripture taken from the Living Bible, copyright © 1971 Tyndale House Publishers. All rights reserved.

Scripture quotations taken from the Life Principles Bible, copyright © 2005 by Charles F. Stanley.

Book Design: Nyesia Mehta

ISBN: 978-0-9817911-0-4

Library of Congress Control Number: 2010910701

Printed in the United States of America

Special Dedication

This book is dedicated to God who worked sanctification in me. I am very grateful to give a special dedication to my spiritual Father Apostle Richard D. Henton who prophesied to me. He said: "You have been asking God are you chosen and God told me 'Yes, yes, yes God has chosen you and he can trust you." Apostle Henton taught on sanctification in many of his messages. He gave me permission to be mentored by the late Dr. Estella Boyd who mentored, trained me and birthed me out as a Daughter of Zion. Dr. Boyd prophesied to me that God had chosen me to be an Elect Lady. Through her training, it elevated me to this level. The main subject of Mother Boyd's handbook is sanctification. Along with many other scriptures to study, she told me when I search it out to obey everything God puts His finger on in my life and God will allow me to do what she was doing. Apostle R. D. Henton would intercede for me during the times I would be on the field with Mother Boyd. I give this special dedication to these anointed vessels God used in my life.

Acknowledgements

God gave the vision to a write this book for the Body of Christ. Many people worked behind the scenes to make this book a reality. I would like to give thanks to several individuals who prayed with me and for me in the birthing of this book:

To my beloved King (husband) Pastor Victor Johnson for 14 years of marriage and commitment. I am very grateful for him joining me in allowing God to sanctify him in the kingdom work of God. He has encouraged and helped me to reach for the stars and comforted me when I didn't feel I could. He is truly the person who encouraged me to go forth and write this book that was birthed in me.

To my son Fred Abernathy, daughter-in-law Monica, and to my two little daughters of Zion (granddaughters) Mekari and Mariah for their unwavering love and commitment. They have been a great encouragement to me.

To my Spiritual Mother Estella Boyd who adopted me as her spiritual daughter. I am very grateful for her and everything that I am and ever desire to be is because she taught me how to keep my hope in God.

To my precious sister in Christ, Janet Faulkner who traveled with me doing Daughters of Zion and Sons of Thunder classes. I thank God for smiling on me by sending you into my life, your faithfulness, love and prayers are unmatched.

To my first Daughters of Zion and Sons of Thunder Class which was a blessing to me to publish my first book.

To my family: six sisters, two brothers, and my late brother Charles and a host of nieces and nephews.

To my spiritual Daughters and Sons, Clara, Deborah, La Tonya, Evangelist Lisa, Theresa, and Priscilla, Son, Willie, Pastor Randall, Minister Dwayne, Vergis, and Lonnie.

To God for the pastors and leaders who allowed me to share my classes with their church. Mother Boyd birthed me out as a Daughter of Zion, so that I would pray for leaders as she did.

Praise for *Pursuing Sanctification*

*All of these ladies are Daughters of Zion.

"Mrs. Elect Lady Vanessa Johnson, through the Holy Spirit, has been given insight and revelation to write this book. She is a teacher, minister, fervent prayer warrior, and one of the most dedicated Christians I know. God has given her a powerful, life changing message that will bless you tremendously. Enjoy this teaching and wisdom that will lead you to eternal life."

-Clarice Plott

"Elect Lady Johnson has touched my life, especially with her teachings with the Daughters of Zion classes. So life changing, she encourages through the Word of Father God. "Let us walk as Daughters of Zion, believing that watchfulness, prayer, fasting and wailing is the only way by which we can get our petition answered from Father God." I can personally acknowledge that Elect Lady Johnson lives her life as a daughter, wife, and mother in Christ Jesus. I believe that this book given to her by the Holy Spirit will challenge all Christians to put aside all selfish desires, and realize that we need Father God to help us do what He needs us to do. His will, not ours! To God Be the Glory."

-Dr. Patricia James-Tate

"I would like to thank the Lord Jesus Christ for anointing Elect Lady Johnson with the wisdom and boldness to put together such and awesome and powerful book that will enlighten the Body of Christ from the HEAD down. In the many years of my knowing Elect Lady Johnson, I have found her to be faithful to the Lord, to the ministry and exemplify a genuine love for God's people. I believe as you read this book you will discover a purity reserved for those who want to live and walk in the fullness of Christ.I take great pleasure in knowing Jesus Christ has raised up a voice in this end time to remind us that sanctification is necessary and available to the people of God. This is not just another book on being sanctified. Pursuing Sanctification is a God-inspired guide on how to know, receive and perform God's will in your life today."

-Evangelist Fannie Shepherd

"This book has been written, inspired, and ordained by the Spirit of God to take on a deeper meaning of sanctification. As we now live in the 21st century, we've allowed the enemy to invade us with so many ungodly distractions. We also seem to have lost determination in continuing to strive for purpose and destiny along the way. I pray that you'll be enlightened, encouraged and strengthened as Elect Lady Johnson shares with us insightful wisdom on being set apart for the end time harvest of souls."

-Anita Overton

"I thank God that Elect Lady Johnson took heed to the command from God to put pen to paper and share with the body of Christ the revelations that God has given her on the need for sanctification and seeking our inheritance from God. Her life of diligently seeking the Lord is a living epistle to Christendom of the wisdom that God will reward to His believers. Her wisdom will aid in illuminating the Word to not only babes in Christ but those veterans of the five fold ministry."

Janet M. Faulkner RN BSN

Table of Contents

- Foreword — i
- Introduction — iii
- 1. Why We Need to Be Sanctified — 7
- 2. The Purpose of Sanctification — 19
- 3. How God Uses Sanctification — 25
- 4. Certain Evils to Avoid — 37
- 5. Sanctification Gives Us Authority — 49
- 6. Doing the Will of God — 67
- 7. Vital Prayer — 81
- 8. Expect to Suffer — 93
- 9. How to Receive Your Real Inheritance from God — 103
- 10. Called to be Blameless — 127
- About the Author — 149
- References — 153

Foreword

For years we have heard and [been] taught that we are living in the last days, that these are the perilous times revealed to us by Paul:

> "This know also, that in the last days perilous times shall come" (2 Timothy 3:1).

We see now, more than ever, that here in the 21st century that teaching was true. The [patriarchs] of our time taught, preached, and lived a higher level of holiness through purification and sanctification. We as the Body of Christ have to recognize the place that we are in so that we may position ourselves and seek His face preparing to see our soon coming King…

> "….of that day and hour knoweth no man, no, not the angels of heaven, by my Father only" (Matthew 24:36).

We have to sanctify ourselves through His truth and the Word of God is the truth. That's why His word was so powerful in the lives of those who stood on it:

> "In the beginning was the Word and the Word was with God, and the Word was God" (John 1:1)

This word that our lives and faith are built on cannot penetrate who we are until we sanctify ourselves. We need the power and comfort of the Holy Ghost to lead, guide and direct our path in this process in which we fully incorporate the spiritual reality of Christ, or being made more like Christ. Righteousness comes by the Word of God and with that combination we can take a closer look into ourselves.

"But let a man examine himself, and so let him eat of that bread, and drink of that cup" (1 Corinthians 11:28)

The teachings and logos of God will then penetrate the core of our beings moving us forward into the spirit of perfection:

"…. Principles of the doctrine of Christ let us go on unto perfection;" (Hebrew 6:1)

God has anointed a vessel [Elect Lady Johnson] for such a time as this to reveal to the saints the principles of God so that we can secure eternal life with Him and be more in tune with God and the things of God. So with an elevated mind and an open heart receive what God has given for us to draw closer to Him.

"He that hath an ear, let him hear what the Spirit saith unto the churches; To him that overcometh will I give to eat of the tree of life, which is in the midst of the paradise of God." (Revelation 2:7)

Apostle Curlin
All Nations House of Prayer
Hopkinsville, Kentucky

Introduction

You must start the process of sanctification in your life. *Sanctification is the setting apart of something or someone to a particular use or service. Theologically it speaks of God setting apart the believer for Himself, from all evil use, to be wholly used for Himself and His service.* The Hebrew word qadesh means *to be clean, to make, pronounce or observe as clean, ceremonially or morally.* It is translated under these words: *consecrate, dedicate, hallow, holy, purity, sanctify.* The Greek word hagiasmos and related Greek words mean *to make holy, purity,* or *consecrate.* They are translated by these words: *sanctify, sanctification, hallow, be holy, holiness.* Sanctification therefore means *to be separate, or to be set apart especially for holy use.*

How It All Began

I was a member of Monument of Faith Church where Apostle Richard D. Henton is founder and Pastor. One Friday while in a shut-in in the prayer room with the late Dr. Estella Boyd, she told me that I have God's love. She also told me that she asked God if she could be my spiritual mother. She discerned that I loved God and the Lord loved me. This is why she told me that God told her to put the veil on me and she adopted me. She then asked me to be her nurse and to travel with her.

> *I love those who love me, and those who seek me early and diligently shall find me. Riches and honor are with me, en-*

during wealth and righteousness (uprightness in every area and relation, and right standing with God). My fruit is better than gold, yes, than refined gold, and my increase than choice silver. (Proverbs 8:17-21 AMP)

In 2000, while sitting at my kitchen table in Cleveland, Ohio, I felt like I was alone on the isle of Patmos. (see Revelation 1:9) I began to accept an opportunity to start teaching Daughters of Zion and Sons of Thunder classes. The teaching ministry of the Daughters of Zion and Sons of Thunder classes was birthed in me through the late Dr. Estella Boyd. 2 Samuel 5:7 says Zion is the city of David. The late Mother Estella Boyd was a Mother in Zion as was Deborah (see Judges 5:7). A Daughter of Zion is birthed out by a righteous Mother of Zion with God as her Father. A Daughter of Zion is first and foremost a virtuous woman (Proverbs 31:10) (*The Daughter of Zion Handbook*). John 12:15 says, *Fear not, Daughter of Sion; behold the King cometh, sitting on an ass's colt.* The New Testament makes reference to the Daughter of Zion from the word of our Lord Jesus Christ. Paul stated in Titus 2:4: *That they may teach the young women to be sober, to love their husbands, to love their children.* One of the first subjects that was birthed in me was sanctification and God began to show me how important it was to be sanctified and set apart for Him. I began to see how important this would be to the Body of Christ.

God opened a door in Cleveland, Ohio for me to teach my first Daughters of Zion and Sons of Thunder class. There were more than sixty people in this class and they were tremendously blessed by it. They allowed God to begin the process of sanctification in them. Sanctification is the work of God in us.

Biblical View of Sanctification

INTRODUCTION

God's view of sanctification is set forth in the Exodus 29. God used Aaron and his sons and set them apart (sanctified them) for God purposes for their lives. Exodus 29:33 says *And they shall eat those things wherewith the atonement was made, to consecrate and to sanctify them: but a stranger shall not eat thereof, because they are holy.* God also sets his sons and daughters today apart for His purpose. God commands His sanctified ones.

> *I have commanded my sanctified ones, I have also called my mighty ones for mine anger, even them that rejoice in my highness (Isaiah 13:3).*

The prophet's views of sanctification:

> *But the Lord of hosts shall be exalted in judgment, and God that is holy shall be sanctified in righteousness (Isaiah 5:16)*

Before the womb, God knew us. Jeremiah 1:5 AMP:

> *Before I formed you in the womb I knew [and] approved of you [as My chosen instrument], and before you were born I separated and set you apart, consecrating you; [and] I appointed you as a prophet to the nations*

Ezekiel 36:23 AMP:

> *And I will vindicate the holiness of My great name and separate it for its holy purpose from all that defiles it--My name, which has been profaned among the nations, which you have profaned among them--and the nations will know, understand, and realize that I am the Lord [the Sovereign Ruler, Who calls forth loyalty and obedient service], when I shall be set apart by you and My holiness vindicated in you before their eyes and yours.*

Jesus viewed sanctification as being performed by God.

John 10:36 AMP [If that is true] do you say of the One Whom the father consecrated and dedicated and set apart for Himself and sent him into the world, You are blaspheming, because I said I am the Son of God?

Sanctification opens the eyes and turns men from darkness to light.

To open their eyes that they may turn from darkness to light and from the power of Satan to God, so that they may thus receive forgiveness and release from their sins and a place and portion among those who are consecrated and purified by faith in Me (Acts 26:18 AMP).

The apostles view of sanctification is that your inheritance is among the sanctified ones which is found in the heart.

And now [brethren], I commit you to God [I deposit you in His charge, entrusting you to His protection and care]. And I commend you to the Word of His grace [to the commands and counsels and promises of His unmerited favor]. It is able to build you up and to give you [your rightful] inheritance among all God's set-apart ones (those consecrated, purified, and transformed of soul) (Acts 20:32 AMP).

But in your hearts set Christ apart as holy [and acknowledge Him] as Lord. Always be ready to give a logical defense to anyone who asks you to account for the hope that is in you, but do it courteously and respectfully 1 Peter 3:15 AMP.

Chapter 1

Why We Need to Be Sanctified

We need to be sanctified because the believer has three major enemies: the world, the flesh, and the devil.

The Enemy of the World

The Greek word for **world** is *kosmos* (kos–mos) which means *orderly arrangement, decoration, a harmonious arrangement or order*. The definition of **world** in *Funk & Wagnalls Dictionary* is *the practices, usages, and ways of men. The course of events as affecting ones personality individual condition or circumstances. Earthly existence mortal life.*

All of us have walked according to the course of this world at some time or another. Some of us were brought up in church and knew the Bible teachings but did not obey them. This is where we allowed the prince of this world to lead our lives. Whenever we are disobedient to the Word of God, we give place to the enemy.

> *Ephesians 2:2,3: Wherein in time past ye walked according to the course of this world, according to the prince of the power of the air, the spirit that now worketh in the children of disobedience: Among whom also we all had our conversation in times past in the lusts of our flesh, fulfilling the desires of the flesh, and of the mind; and were by nature the*

children of wrath, even as others.

Take special note to verse 27 of Ephesians 4. It states clearly that we should give no opportunity or place to Satan.

Leave no [such] room or foothold for the devil [give no opportunity to him]. Let the thief steal no more, but rather let him be industrious, making an honest living with his own hands, so that he may be able to give to those in need. Let no foul or polluting language, nor evil word nor unwholesome or worthless talk [ever] come out of your mouth, but only such [speech] as is good and beneficial to the spiritual progress of others, as is fitting to the need and the occasion, that it may be a blessing and give grace (God's favor) to those who hear it. And do not grieve the Holy Spirit of God [do not offend or vex or sadden Him], by Whom you were sealed (marked, branded as God's own, secured) for the day of redemption (of final deliverance through Christ from evil and the consequences of sin). Let all bitterness and indignation and wrath (passion, rage, bad temper) and resentment (anger, animosity) and quarreling (brawling, clamor, contention) and slander (evil-speaking, abusive or blasphemous language) be banished from you, with all malice (spite, ill will, or baseness of any kind). And become useful and helpful and kind to one another, tenderhearted (compassionate, understanding, loving-hearted), forgiving one another (readily and freely), as God in Christ forgave you (Ephesians 4:27-32 AMP).

Our evil lust and desires cause contentions and which show that we walk in strife and carnality. One of the main reasons God wants us to see that the world system is an enemy is because of covetousness. The origin of wars is covetousness which is the desire to get that which belongs to others (Halley's Bible Handbook). James 4:1: *From whence* come wars and fightings among you? come they not hence, even of your lusts that war in your members?

We can read further in James 4:2-7 AMP:

> *You are jealous and covet [what others have] and your desires go unfulfilled; [so] you become murderers. [To hate is to murder as far as your hearts are concerned.] You burn with envy and anger and are not able to obtain (the gratification, the contentment, and the happiness that you seek), so you fight and war. You do not have, because you do not ask. [Or] you do ask [God for them] and yet fail to receive, because you ask with wrong purpose and evil, selfish motives. Your intention is [when you get what you desire] to spend it in sensual pleasures. You [are like] unfaithful wives (having illicit love affairs with the world and breaking your marriage vow to God)! Do you not know that being the world's friend is being God's enemy? So whoever chooses to be a friend of the world takes his stand as an enemy of God. Or do you suppose that the Scripture is speaking to no purpose that says, The Spirit Whom He has caused to dwell in us yearns over us and He yearns for the Spirit (to be welcome) with a jealous love? But He gives us more and more grace (power of the Holy Spirit, to meet this evil tendency and all others fully). That is why He says, God sets Himself against the proud and haughty, but gives grace [continually] to the lowly (those who are humble enough to receive it). So be subject to God. Resist the devil [stand firm against him], and he will flee from you.*

When we are humble to God, it takes care of worldliness. Timothy talks of Demas, a person having loved the world actually loved an enemy and an enemy will never lead you the right way. *For Demas has deserted me for love of this present world and has gone to Thessalonica; Crescens [has gone] to Galatia, Titus to Dalmatia* (2 Timothy 4:10 AMP). There are warnings against worldliness. God does not want us to be devoted to lust and pleasure because it is used by the evil world of men.

> *1 John 2:15-17 AMP: Do not love or cherish the world or the things that are in the world. If anyone loves the world, love for the Father in not in him. For all that is in the world-the lust of the flesh [craving for sensual gratification] and the lust of the eyes [greedy longings of the mind] and the pride of life [assurance in one's own resources or in the stability of earthly things]-these do not come from the father but are from the world [itself]. And the world passes away and disappears, and with it the forbidden cravings [passionate desires, the lust] of it; but he who does the will of God and carries out His purposes in his life abides [remains] forever.*

The Enemy of the Flesh

According to Funk & Wagnalls, flesh means *the body of man as opposed to the soul or spirit; also physical, sensual nature of man as distinguished from or opposed to the spiritual or intellectual nature. All flesh must die. Fleshy.* The Greek word for flesh is *sarx which* means *carnal, carnally minded, fleshly.*

We all are weak because of the flesh; therefore weakness is a problem of the flesh, not of the law. Our flesh is not the human body, but it is our old nature that has the tendency to sin. The inward man struggles with sinful desires. *All of you must keep awake (give strict attention, be cautious and active) and watch and pray, that you may not come into temptation. The spirit indeed is willing, but the flesh is weak* (Matthew 26:41 AMP). God has created mankind with built in weakness that we all might learn to lean and trust in Him.

For I know that in me (that is, in my flesh,) dwelleth no good thing... (Romans 7:18). This makes you think of your own ability or rather, the lack thereof, in comparison to the Holy Spirit, especially when it comes to spiritual things. Paul is saying here how most modern Christians try to live for God by their own power, but how to perform that which is good I find not. Without being sanctified it is impossible to find a way to do good. We don't have the power by ourselves to do what pleases God, even the good things.

Here are some scripture references regarding man's fallen nature:

Isaiah 64:6: But we are all as an unclean thing, and all our righteousness are as filthy rags; and we do all fade as a leaf; and our iniquities, like the wind, have taken us away.

Romans 7:12: Wherefore the law is holy, and the commandment holy, and just, and good.

Romans 7:13-24 (Living Bible): But how can that be? Didn't the law cause my doom? How then can it be good? No, it was sin, devilish stuff that it is, that used what was good to bring about my condemnation. So you can see how cunning and deadly and damnable it is. For it uses God's good laws for its own evil purposes. The law is good, then, and the trouble is not there but with me, because I am sold into slavery with sin as my owner. I don't understand myself at all, for I really want to do what is right, but I can't. I do what I don't want to-what I hate. I know perfectly well that what I am doing is wrong, and my bad conscience proves that I agree with these laws I am breaking. But I can't help myself, because I am no longer doing it. It is sin inside me that is stronger than I am that makes me do these evil things. I know that I am rotten through and through so far

> as my old sinful nature is concerned. No matter which way I turn I can't make myself do right. I want to but I can't. When I want to do good, I don't; and when I try not to do wrong, I do it anyway. Now if I am doing what I don't want to; it is plain where the trouble is: sin still has its evil grasp. It seems to be a fact of life that when I want to do what is right, I inevitably do what is wrong. I love to do God's will so far as my new nature is concerned; but there is something else deep within me, in my lower nature, that is at war with my mind and wins the fight and makes me a slave to the sin that is still within me. In my mind I want to be God's willing servant but instead I still find myself enslaved to sin. So you see how it is: my new life tells me to do right, but the old nature that is still inside me loves to sin. Oh, what a terrible predicament I am in! Who will free me from my slavery to this deadly lower nature? Thank God! It has been done by Jesus Christ our Lord. He has set me free.

The Bible reveals to us the character of God. His holiness, righteousness, justice, goodness, kindness, etc. is the image of Him. The Bible both proclaims his perfect nature and manifest to us our own fallen nature. (Life Principles Bible) God has a solution to the problem of the flesh and the carnal mind.

> But I say, walk and live [habitually] in the [Holy] Spirit [responsive to and controlled and guided by the Spirit]; then you will certainly not gratify the cravings and desires of the flesh (of human nature without God). For the desires of the flesh are opposed the [Holy] Spirit, and the [desires of the] Spirit are opposed to the flesh (godless human nature); for these are antagonistic to each other [continually withstanding and in conflict with each other], so that you are not free but are prevented from doing what you desire to do (Galatians 5:16-17 AMP).

> *I advise you to obey only the Holy Spirit's instructions. He will tell you where to go and what to do, and then you won't always be doing the wrong things your evil nature wants you to. For we naturally love to do evil things that are just the opposite from things that the Holy Spirit tells us to do; and the good things we want to do when the Spirit has his way with us are just the opposite of our natural desires. These two forces within us are constantly fighting each other to win control over us, and our wishes are never free from their pressures. (Galatians 5:16-17 Living Bible)*

There are things will help us to mortify the flesh; we must set our affections on things above (Colossians 3:1-9):

> *If ye then be risen with Christ, seek those things which are above, where Christ sitteth on the right hand of God. Set your affections on things above, not on things on the earth. For ye are dead, and your life is hid with Christ in God. When Christ, who is our life, shall appear, then ye also shall appear with him in glory. Mortify therefore your members which are upon the earth; fornication, uncleanness, inordinate affections, evil concupiscence, and covetousness, which is idolatry: For which things' sake the wrath of God cometh upon the children of disobedience: In the which ye also walked some times, when ye lived in them. But now ye also put off all these; anger, wrath, malice, blasphemy, filthy communication out of your mouth. Lie not one to another, seeing that ye have put off the old man with his deeds;*

According to *Webster's Dictionary,* affection means *fond attachment, inclination of mind or tendency.* The Greek word for affection is *phroneo* which means *to exercise the mind, entertain or have a sentiment or opinion, to interest oneself in.*

Kevin J.Conner has some excellent notes on Romans 8:5-9.

Verse 5: *For they that are after the flesh do mind the things of the flesh; but they that are after the spirit the things of the spirit*

The mind

After the flesh: meaning the things of the flesh; fleshly things.

After the Spirit: meaning things of the Spirit, spiritual things (John 3:6; Galatians 5:22).

Verse 6: *For to be carnally minded is death; but to be spiritually minded is life and peace.*

The mind

Carnally minded: (carnivorous) results in death

Spiritually minded: results in life and peace (Refer to Romans 7:14 on the word "carnal.")

The battle is a battle of the mind. One is either minding the flesh or minding the spirit.

Verse 7: *Because the carnal mind is enmity against God: for it is not subject to the law of God, neither indeed can be.*

The Carnal Mind

Enmity against God: a rebel at war against God

Not subject to the law of God: lawless

Neither indeed can be: resists God (James 4:4; 1 Corinthians 2:14; battle of the mind)

Verse 8: *So then they that are in the flesh cannot please God*

In the flesh

In the flesh: represents a sinful, carnal nature that cannot please God. This phrase compared with "in Adam." In contrast "in the Spirit" refers to walking, moving, and obeying the Spirit of God according to the Word. This phrase compares with ''In Christ."

Verse 9: *But ye are not in the flesh, but in the Spirit, if so be that the Spirit of God dwells in you. Now if any man have not the Spirit of Christ he is none of his.*

A. ''In the flesh": Being "in the flesh" is to follow after the evil desires of the fallen nature.

B." In the Spirit" (Revelations 1:10; 4:2; Galatians 4:6): Being in the Spirit" is to follow after the will, thoughts, and the desires of the Spirit of God and the Word. These terms are often misunderstood in Christianity. "In the Spirit" is not some *mystical* realm. Jesus and the apostles were naturally spiritual and spiritually natural. They were normal men that lived in the Spirit and had the life of the Spirit.

C. "The Spirit": Note the emphasis on the Holy Spirit in this verse and in the entire chapter. In this chapter, "I" is mentioned two times, "sin" three times, "Lord" nine times, "Holy Spirit" twenty-one times, and "law" four times. In Romans seven to emphasis is "I". In Romans 8, the emphasis is:
- "the Spirit" (Romans 8:1-2,4,9-11,13-16,23,26-27)

- Spiritually (verse 6)
- Spiritual bondage (verse 15)
- Our Spirit (verse 16)

Our Enemy the Devil

Webster's New World Dictionary says the word *Devil* means *any of the evil spirits of hell in religious belief and in folk tales, especially the devil, the chief devil, the chief evil spirit, who is also called Satan, he is usually shown as a man with horns, a forked tail etc. An evil or cruel person or spirit.* The definition in Funk and Wagnalls Dictionary is *in Jewish and Christian theology, the prince and ruler of the kingdom of evil. Satan. A demon. Christian science usage, evil, a lie; error; neither corporeality nor mind, opposite of truth.* The Greek word for devil is *diabolos* which means *a traducer, false accuser, slander.*

Here is the biblical account of the Devil's fall from Heaven:

> *Moreover the word of the Lord came unto me, saying, Son of man, take up a lamentation upon the king of Tyrus, and say unto him, Thus saith the Lord GOD; Thou sealest up the sum, full of wisdom and perfect in beauty. Thou hast been in Eden the garden of God; every precious stone was thy covering, the sardius, topaz, and the diamond, the beryl, the onyx, and the jasper, the sapphire, the emerald, and the carbuncle, and gold: the workmanship of thy tabrets and of thy pipes was prepared in thee in the day that thou wast created. Thou art the anointed cherub that covereth; and I have set thee so: thou wast upon the holy mountain of God; thou hast walked up and down in the midst of the stones of fire. Thou wast perfect in thy ways from the day thou wast created, till iniquity was found in thee. By the multitude of thy merchandise they have filled the midst of thee with violence, and thou hast sinned: therefore I will cast thee*

as profane out of the mountain of God: and I will destroy thee, O covering cherub, from the midst of the stones of fire. Thine heart was lifted up because of thy beauty, thou hast corrupted thy wisdom by reason of thy brightness: I will cast thee to the ground, I will lay thee before kings, that they may behold thee. Thou hast defiled thy sanctuaries, by the multitude of thine iniquities, by the iniquity of thy traffick; therefore will I bring forth a fire from the midst of thee, it shall devour thee, and I will bring thee to ashes upon the earth in the sight of all them that behold thee. All they that know thee among the people shall be astonished at thee: thou shalt be a terror, and never shalt thou be any more. (Ezekiel 28:11-19)

We need to use the word of God to sanctify us, so God can remove our weaknesses and replace them with His strength. We can overcome just as Jesus did when He was tempted by the Devil.

Then JESUS was led (guided) by the [Holy] Spirit into the wilderness (desert) to be tempted (tested and tried) by the devil. And He went without food for forty days and forty nights, and later He was hungry. [Exodus 34:28; 1 Kings 19:8] And the tempter came and said to Him, If You are God's Son, command these stones to be made [loaves of] bread. But He replied, It has been written, Man shall not live and be upheld and sustained by bread alone, but by every word that comes forth from the mouth of God. [Deuteronomy 8:3] Then the devil took Him into the holy city and place Him on a turret (pinnacle, gable) of the temple sanctuary. [Nehemiah 11:1; Daniel 9:24] And he said to Him, If You are the Son of God, throw Yourself down; for it is written, He will give His angels charge over you, and they will bear you up on their hands, lest you strike your foot against a stone. [Psalm 91:11,12] Jesus said to him, On the other hand, it is written also, You shall not tempt, test thoroughly, or try exceedingly the Lord your God. [Deuteronomy 6:16] Again, the devil took Him up on a very high mountain and showed Him all the kingdoms of the world and the glory (the splendor, magnificence, preeminence, and excellence) of them. And he said to Him, These things, all taken together, I will give You, if You will prostrate Yourself before me and do homage and worship me. Then Jesus said to him, Be gone, Satan! For it has been written. You shall worship the Lord your God, and Him alone shall you serve. [Deuteronomy 6:13] Then the devil departed from Him, and behold, angels came and ministered to Him (Matthew 4:1-11 AMP).

Jesus is our greatest example. We can face our enemy, the Devil, by pursuing sanctification in our own personal wilderness. After Jesus' baptism by John, the Holy Spirit led Jesus out into the wilderness. Jesus shows us we can prepare ourselves to be used by God through a wilderness experience. We can deal with wilderness experience better and can see that it could be part of our preparation to be used by Him. It will purify our motives, make our back bones firm, and profession clear. So temptation can be defeated if we stand on what Jesus did. He stood on the Word, "It is written," and He never lost. This could be a way of God testing us. Jesus shows us not to let Satan make us doubt the Word of God and what He said is true. This is why we need to know what the Word says. Exodus 15:9 tells of the great need to be sanctified:

The enemy said, I will pursue, I will overtake, I will divide the spoil; my lust shall be satisfied upon them; I will draw my sword, my hand shall destroy them.

Chapter 2

The Purpose of Sanctification

Funk and Wagnalls defines *purpose* as *an idea or deal kept before the mind as an end of effort or action; plan; design; aim. Settled resolution; determination; goal.* The Synonym Finder gives these synonyms for *purpose*: *Reason, point, why, principle, guiding principle, ultimate aim; expectation, expect outcome, anticipation, outlook, prospect; vision, hope, steadfastness, ambition, drive, diligent, industry, persistence, constancy, perseverance, stand firm, stick to one's guns, elect, head.* The Greek word for purpose is *prothesis* which is *a setting forth, proposal (intention), one puts forth his purpose then acts.*

It is important to be separated from others for God's purpose as Israel was separated from the heathen to be joined with God.

> *You shall therefore make a distinction between the clean beast and the unclean, and between the unclean fowl and the clean; and you shall not make yourselves detestable with beast or with bird or with anything with which the ground teems or that creeps, which I have set apart from you as unclean. And you shall be holy to Me; for I the Lord am holy, and have separated you from the peoples, that you should be Mine (Leviticus 20:25-26 AMP).*

You can also see that the Lord reassures Jeremiah that if he would separate, he will be God's mouthpiece.

Therefore thus says the Lord [to Jeremiah]: If you return [and give up this mistaken tone of distrust and despair], then I will give you again a settled place of quiet and safety, and you be My minister; and if you separate the precious from the vile [cleansing your own heart from unworthy and unwarranted suspicions concerning God's faithfulness], you shall be My mouthpiece. [But do not yield to them.] Let them return to you-not you to [the people] (Jeremiah 15:19 AMP).

In verses 19-21 of the 15th Chapter of Jeremiah (Maxwell Leader Bible), God gave the prophet Jeremiah courage by giving him a:

1. Picture of Himself: God allowed him to stand and see a vision of Yahweh.
2. Picture of the people: God confirms Jeremiah's view that people are stubborn.
3. Picture of victory: God reminds him that the Lord is greater than any circumstance.

It is an exclusive, honorable and tremendous responsibility to belong to God. We cannot have this without a personal relationship and holy life.

Exodus 33:16: For wherein shall it be known here that I and thy people have found grace in thy sight? Is it not in that thou goest with us? so shall we be separated, I and thy people, from all the people that are upon the face of the earth.

This scripture lets others know the difference in you when God sanctifies you and separates you from all the people upon the earth. Being separated for God, you shall not be reckoned and esteemed among the nation.

THE PURPOSE OF SANCTIFICATION

Numbers 23:9 AMP: For from the top of the rocks I see Israel, and from the hills I behold him. Behold, the people [of Israel] shall dwell alone and shall not be reckoned and esteemed among the nations.

And Joshua said to the people, Sanctify yourselves [that is, separate yourselves for a special holy purpose], for tomorrow the Lord will do wonders among you (Joshua 3:5 AMP).

God does not need us to comprehend His will, just to obey it, even if it seems irrational, because when God sanctifies us He can use all temperament and backgrounds to accomplish His purpose and do wonders. When we are separated [set apart] for God's purpose, He will reassure us as he did with Jeremiah. He was neglected, mistreated and lonely. He endured continual discouragement and he felt let down by God.

I believe if we accept God's purpose of sanctifying us we can see clearly as well. God gets all the Glory, when he can see men and women after His own heart. This comes through great sacrifice to Him, as David did. *And he said, Peaceably; I am come to sacrifice unto the Lord: sanctify yourselves, and come with me to the sacrifice. And he sanctified Jesse and his sons, and called them to the sacrifice (*1 Samuel 16:5). David loved the Lord and lived his life as a man after God's own heart.

Another purpose for sanctification is to prepare us to be used by God. God wanted someone to speak for him; He had a message and was looking for messenger. I believe Isaiah took it personally as seen in Isaiah 6:1-8.

In the year that King Uz-zi'ah died I saw also the Lord sitting upon a throne, high and lifted up, and his train filled the temple. Above it stood the seraphims: each one had six wings; with twain he covered his face, and with twain he covered his fee, and with twain he did fly. And one cried unto another, and said, Holy, holy, holy, is the Lord of hosts: the whole earth is full of his glory. And the posts of the door moved at the voice of him that cried, and the house was filled with smoke. Then said I, Woe is me! For I am undone; because I am a man of unclean lips and I dwell in the midst of a people of unclean lips, and I dwell in the midst of a people of unclean lips: for mine eyes have seen the King, the Lord of hosts. Then flew one of the seraphims unto me, having a live coal in his hand, which he had taken with the tongs from off the altar: And he laid it upon my mouth, and said, Lo, this hath touched thy lips; and thine iniquity is taken away, and thy sin purged. Also I heard the voice of the Lord, saying, Whom shall I send, and who will go for us? Then said I, Here am I; send me.

Isaiah saw a heavenly vision and beholds the Glory of things to come.

Psalm 17:15: As for me, I will behold thy face in righteousness: I shall be satisfied, when I awake, with thy likeness.

Here we can see that Isaiah accepted the call which was favorable for God's purpose. He had the skill of being able to accomplish the tasks. He also had the willingness to obey and consecrate to God. I believe we are in the day of God's power so we must begin to pursue sanctification. God said in Psalm 110:3:

Thy people shall be willing in the day of thy power, in the beauties of holiness from the womb of the morning: thou hast the dew of thy youth.

THE PURPOSE OF SANCTIFICATION

Isaiah 1:19: If ye be willing and obedient, ye shall eat the good of the land:

My mentor Dr. Estella Boyd would tell us that every one of God's "shalls" is loaded. Pursuing sanctification changed my whole life when I saw the holiness which God had bestowed upon me. When I first began to study sanctification in depth, His awesome presence came upon me and I began to weep. Even as I am writing this part in the book, I'm feeling His presence to the very core of my soul. I cried out "I surrender all to the Lord, sanctify me in and out and I will do your will".

I believe we will never deal thoroughly with our sin without first having a real relationship with God, getting to know who He is. When we study His Word and obey it, we can grasp His holiness and reverence Him in our hearts. We should be like Isaiah, who knew how to humble himself before God. We must understand that we fall far short of His holiness. My mentor told me that you cannot live above sin, but you can live from sin, if you are willing to obey His Word. She said God keeps the saints. We search the scriptures about God:

- The Pilgrim's Companion: Genesis 28:15
- The Sleepless Watchman: Psalm 121:4
- The Protecting Father: John 17:11
- The Almighty Guardian: 2 Timothy 1:12

Another purpose of sanctification is to make us whole: our emotions, spirits, soul and body, ready for Christ's return.

1 Thessalonians 5:17-24 AMP: Be unceasing in prayer [praying persevering], Thank [God] in everything [no mat-

> ter what the circumstance may be, be thankful and give thanks], for this is the will of God for you [who are] in Christ Jesus [the Revealer and Mediator of that will]. Do not quench (suppress or subdue) the [Holy] Spirit; Do not spurn the gifts and utterances of the prophets [do not depreciate prophetic revelations nor despise inspired instruction or exhortation or warning]. But test and prove all things [until you can recognize] what is good; [to that] hold fast. Abstain from evil [shrink from it and keep aloof from it] in whatever form or whatever kind it may be. And may the God of peace Himself sanctify you through and through [separate you from profane things, make you pure and wholly consecrated to God]; and may your spirit and soul and body be preserved sound and complete [and found] blameless at the coming of our Lord Jesus Christ (the Messiah). Faithful is He Who is calling you [to Himself] and utterly trustworthy, and He will also do it [fulfill His call by hallowing and keeping you].

Another purpose for sanctification is to make all things new in our life.

> And I saw the holy city, the new Jerusalem, descending out of heaven from God, all arrayed like a bride beautified and adorned for her husband (Revelations 21:2 AMP).

Chapter 3

How God Uses Sanctification

We must keep God's statutes and commandments. Statutes means: representation, likeness; image, head, figure, ordinances or law. The Greek word for statute is chuggah which means regulation, prescription. Commandment means to order, require or enjoin with authority; to overlook something from a superior position.

When the believers keep his statutes and do them, He is the One who sanctifies them. This is why we should keep God's statutes and commandments because when we do not there is a penalty for breaking the law.

Therefore shall ye observe all my statutes, and all my judgments, and do them: I am the Lord (Leviticus 19:37).

And said, If thou wilt diligently hearken to the voice of the Lord thy God, and wilt do that which is right in his sight, and wilt give ear to his commandments, and keep all his statutes, I will put none of these diseases upon thee, which I have brought upon the Egyptians: for I am the Lord that healeth thee (Exodus 15:26; see also Leviticus 26:46).

Behold, I have taught you statutes and judgments, even as the Lord my God commanded me, that ye should do so in the land whither ye go to possess it. (Deuteronomy 4:5; see also

Deuteronomy 16:12)

And if thou wilt walk in my ways, to keep my statutes and my commandments, as thy father David did walk, then I will lengthen thy days (1 Kings 3:14).

The statutes of the Lord are right, rejoicing the heart: the commandment of the Lord is pure, enlightening the eyes. (Psalm 19:8; see also Psalm 119:12,54)

We must keep God's commandments always.

Deuteronomy 6:6 And these words, which I command thee this day, shall be in thine heart:

Deuteronomy 11:8: Therefore shall ye keep all the commandments which I command you this day, that ye may be strong, and go in and possess the land, whither ye go to possess it;

Psalm 119:6: Then shall I not be ashamed, when I have respect unto all thy commandments.

Matthew 15:3 But he answered and said unto them, Why do ye also transgress the commandments of God by your tradition?

The Greatest Commandment

We must follow the greatest commandment if we are to be sanctified.

Matthew 22:36-38 Master, which is the great commandment in the law? Jesus said unto him, Thou shalt love the Lord thy God with all thy heart, and with all thy soul, and with all thy mind. This is the first and great commandment.

1 John 5:3 For this is the love of God, that we keep his commandments: and his commandments are not grievous.

Each period has its divine law. God gave the Ten Commandments to Israel (see Exodus 20: 1-17; Romans 10:4), with death as the penalty for disobedience, (see Numbers 15:32-36; Hebrews 10:28). The law, which "worketh wrath," (Romans 4:15) was given to bring man to Christ (Galatians 3:19-24).

When we obey God's statutes, commandments and laws we will see how He sanctifies us.

Sanctify yourselves therefore, and be ye holy: for I am the Lord your God. And ye shall keep my statutes, and do them: I am the Lord which sanctify you (Leviticus 20:7-8).

We cannot sanctify ourselves and neither could Israel sanctify themselves; it can only happen by obeying God. We should get in the Word of God and let it get in our hearts and our faith will strengthen in what Christ's sacrifice did for us.

When we as sanctified believers keep God's statutes and commandments, it brings obedience and a hearing ear.

Matthew 13:16-17: But blessed (happy, fortunate, and to be envied) are your eyes because they do see, and your ears because they do hear. Truly I tell you, many prophets and righteous men [men who were upright and in right standing with God] yearned to see what you see, and did not see it, and to hear what you hear, and did not hear it.

After writing these scriptures, I was reminded of a prophecy that was give to me by Apostle Garfield Curlin in Hopkinsville, Kentucky. It was during one of the times I was traveling with my mentor Dr. Estella Boyd. We would go every second weekend. He told me that "It was God and you alone, you and God alone. You are going deep, deep, you and God alone. Truth, truth, truth."

Not long after that prophecy, God began to show me things that I did not understand then. I went to Mother Boyd and asked her why God showed me things I did not know. She gave Isaiah 48:5-6 AMP:

Therefore I have declared things to come from of old; before they came to pass I announced them to you, so that you could not say, my idol has done them, and my graven image and my molten image have commanded them. You have heard [these things foretold], now you see this fulfillment, And will you not bear witness to it? I show you specified new things from this time forth, even hidden things [kept in reserve] which you have not known.

I began to share with Mother the things that happened to me when I was born. I turned three shades of colors: gray, pink and yellow. I was born at home and the doctor had to put me in the oven at least three times. My mother told me she had to sleep very close to me to keep temperature around me. My sisters and brothers would tease me and tell that I was baked in the family. My mother told me, as the seventh child, I was born with a veil over me.

I had a dream when I was in the seventh grade and saw three big detectives at my house to take my mother away. I was afraid to come home for lunch because I thought she would be gone. I asked my friend to stop by my house and see if my mother was there. When I got home my mother asked me why I didn't come home for lunch and I began to tell her my dream and she told me that two big detectives came to question her about a shooting. There were many other things God showed me and I would tell her and then they would come to pass.

Chastisement a Mark of Sonship

The sanctified believers who desire to know the Lord in an even greater way are willing to accept His chastening when we do not keep His statutes and commandments.

And have you [completely] forgotten the divine word of appeal and encouragement in which you are reasoned with and addressed as son? My son, do not think lightly or scorn to submit to the correction and discipline of the Lord, nor lose courage and give up and faint when you are reproved or corrected by Him; For the Lord corrects and disciplines everyone whom He loves, and He punishes, even scourges, every son whom He accepts and welcomes to His heart and cherishes. You must submit to and endure [correction] for discipline; God is dealing with you as with sons. For what son is there whom his father does not [thus] train and correct and discipline? Now if you are exempt from correction and left without discipline in which all [of God's children] share, then you are illegitimate offspring and not true sons [at all]. Moreover, we have had earthly fathers who disciplined us and we yielded [to them] and respected [them for training us]. Shall we not much more cheerfully submit to the Father of spirits and so [truly] live? For [our earthly fathers] disciplined us for only a short period of time and chastised us as seemed proper and good to them; but He disciplines us for our certain good, that we may become sharers in His own holiness. For the time being no discipline brings joy, but seems grievous and painful; but afterwards it yields a peaceable fruit of righteousness to those who have been trained by it [a harvest of fruit which consists in righteousness-in conformity to God's will in purpose, thought, and action, resulting in right living and right standing with God]. (Hebrews 12:5-11 AMP)

We know that no one enjoys discipline because it does not feel good; it does not make you smile or happy at first. However, when we accept the correction, blessing always follows. All natural parents would discipline their children to lead them the correct way.

Sanctified Through the Word

Jesus sanctified Himself and continued to pray that we are sanctified by the truth. John 17:14-17 AMP states:

I have given and delivered to them Your word (message) and the world hated them, because they are not of the world [do not belong to the world], just as I am not of the world. I do not ask that You will take them out of the world, but that You will keep and protect them from the evil one. They are not of the world (worldly, belonging to the world), [just] as I am not of the world. Sanctify them [purify, consecrate, separate them for Yourself, make them holy] by the Truth; Your Word is Truth.

From these scriptures, we can see that we have an endowment forever. We must obey the Word because we need to know that Satan rules the spirit of the world and the prince of darkness, so he is a great enemy toward the Lord. As sanctified believers, we should be lights in the darkness of this world. Jesus points out how He keeps us from evil influences of the world: through prayer for the church that it may be kept pure. John 15:3 AMP states *You are cleansed and pruned already, because of the word which I have given you [the teachings I have discussed with you].* We know that this is done through Jesus and our faith in the finished work.

We are the Church

We must realize that we are the church. Paul brings it out in Ephesians 5:21-27:

Submitting yourselves one to another in the fear of God. Wives, submit yourselves unto your own husbands, as unto the Lord. For the husband is the head of the wife, even as Christ is the head of the church: and he is the saviour of the body. Therefore as the church is subject unto Christ, so let the wives be to their own husbands in everything. Husbands, love your wives, even as Christ also loved the church, and gave himself for it; That he might sanctify and cleanse it with the washing of water by the word, That he might present it to himself a glorious church, not having spot, or wrinkle, or any such thing; but that it should be holy and without blemish.

Verse 26 shows us the final presentation of the Church in perfect holiness at the coming Great Day, with the washing of the water by the Word (the Word washes and cleanses one exactly as water).

The hearing of the spoken word causes you to be cleansed, when mixed with faith. Hebrews 4:1-2 AMP:

Therefore, while the promise of entering His rest still holds and is offered [today], let us be afraid [to distrust it], lest any of you should think he has come too late and has come short of [reaching] it. For indeed we have had the glad tid-

ings [Gospel of God] proclaimed to us just as truly as they [the Israelites of old did when the good news of deliverance from bondage came to them]; but the message they heard did not benefit them, because it was not mixed with faith (with the leaning of the entire personality on God in absolute trust and confidence in His power, wisdom, and goodness) by those who heard it; neither were they united in faith with the ones [Joshua and Caleb] who heard (did believe).

The believer must see the need for sanctification by constantly exercising faith in Christ. Sanctification is definitely a process; we will then have the ability and strength to say a real "Yes" to Christ and say "No" to the things of this world. If we do not let this process of sanctification work in us, it will be impossible to find a way to do good.

Romans 7:18 AMP: For I know that nothing good dwells within me, that is, in my flesh, I can will what is right, but I cannot perform it. [I have the intention and urge to do what is right, but no power to carry it out].

We can see as sanctified believers that 1 John 2:15-17 AMP says:

Do not love or cherish the world or the things that are in the world. If anyone loves the world, love for the Father is not in him. For all that is in the world....the lust of the flesh [craving for sensual gratification] and the lust of the eyes [greedy longings of the mind] and the pride of life [assurance in one's own resources or in the stability of earthly things]- these do not come from the Father but are from the world [itself]. And the world passes away and disappears, and with it the forbidden cravings (the passionate desires, the lust) of it; but he who does the will of God and carries out His purpose in his life abides (remains) forever.

John lets us know the ordered system of which Satan is the head. If any man loves the world, the love of the Father is not in him.

Christ's Sacrificial Blood

We have access to so much through the Blood of Christ.

Therefore Jesus also suffered and died outside the [city's] gate in order that He might purify and consecrate the people through [the shedding of] His own blood and set them apart as holy [for God] (Hebrews 13:12 AMP).

For if [the mere] sprinkling of unholy and defiled persons with blood of goats and bulls and with the ashes of a burnt heifer is sufficient for the purification of the body, How much more surely shall the blood of Christ, Who by virtue of [His] eternal Spirit [His own preexistent divine personality] has offered Himself as an unblemished sacrifice to God, purify our consciences from dead works and lifeless observances from to serve the [ever] living God? (Hebrews 9:13-14 AMP; see also Leviticus 16:6,16; Numbers 19:9,17,18).

But if we [really] are living and walking in the Light, as He [Himself] is in the Light, we have [true, unbroken] fellowship with one another, and the blood of Jesus Christ His Son cleanses (removes) us from all sin and guilt [keeps us cleansed from sin in all its forms and manifestations] (1 John 1:7 AMP)

A song from the New National Baptist Hymnal (1977) *Are You Washed In The Blood* is very appropriate here:

Have you been to Jesus for the cleansing pow'r ?
Are you washed in the blood of the Lamb?

Are you ful-ly trust-ing in His grace this hour?
Are you washed in the blood of the Lamb?
Are you washed In the blood washed in the blood of the Lamb?
  In the soul-cleansing blood of the Lamb? Are your garments spotless? Of the Lamb?

No other sacrifice can cleanse our sin, but the blood of Christ. *Halley's Bible Handbook* speaks on the Blood basically in the book of Revelations:

- "Washed from our Sins in His Blood" (1:5).
- "Saved by the Blood of Christ": another emphasis of this book.
- "Thou hast redeemed us to God by Thy Blood" (5:9).
- "They overcome him (Satan) by the Blood of Lamb" (12:11).
- "These are they who ... have Washed their Robes, and made them white in the Blood of the Lamb" (7:14).
- "Blessed are they that Wash their Robes, that they may have the right to the Tree of Life" (22:14).
- There are fastidious intellectuals who rebel at the thought of it. But it is an unbroken Biblical teaching, emphasized again and again in the New Testament. And how it touches our hearts! And how we love and adore Him for it and will through endless acons of Eternity!

We must love the Lord and we must love the Word. We must realize that through the Holy Spirit, sanctified believers can stand firm. 2 Thessalonians 2:13-17 AMP:

But we, brethren beloved by the Lord, ought and are obligated [as those who are in debt] to give thanks always to God for you, because God chose you from the beginning as His firstfruits (first converts) for salvation through the sanc-

tifying work of the [Holy] Spirit and [your] belief in (adherence to, trust in, and reliance on) the Truth. [It was] to this end that He called you through our Gospel, so that you may obtain and share in the glory of our Lord Jesus Christ (the Messiah). So then, brethren, stand firm and hold fast to the traditions and instructions which you were taught by us, whether by our word of mouth or by letter. Now may our Lord Jesus Christ Himself and God our Father, Who loved us and gave us everlasting consolation and encouragement and well-founded hope through [His] grace (unmerited favor) Comfort and encourage your hearts and strengthen them [make them steadfast and keep them unswerving] in every good work and word.

Chapter 4

Certain Evils to Avoid

E<i>vil means morally bad; wicked, evil deeds, causing injury, damage or any other undesirable results, harmful, evil habits, wrong doing, wickedness, etc.</i>

Dr. Boyd taught us by example to avoid certain evils, she showed character and convictions. To ensure the new generation entered the promised land with solid moral guidelines, Moses repeats the commands he gave earlier in Exodus 20. Former general Norman Schwarzkopf put it this way: "Leadership is a potent combination of character and strategy. But if you must be without one, be without strategy." (The Maxwell Leadership Bible).

The Perils of Adultery

Adultery means: The voluntary sexual intercourse of a married person with someone not the spouse, unfaithfulness, in the Bible; Idolatry. The Greek word for adultery is *moicheuo* (moy-khayoo-o) which means: to commit adultery. Metaphorically, of those who are Jezebel's solicitations; drawn away to idolatry. Moichos, moykhos, means: a male paramour, denotes one who has unlawful intercourse with another. *Idolatry* means: *The worship of idols, excessive or undiscerning, admiration or awe or relevance.*

And why wilt thou, my son, be ravished with a strange

woman, and embrace the bosom of a stranger? For the ways of man are before the eyes of the Lord, and he pondereth all his goings. His own iniquities shall take the wicked himself, and he shall be holden with the cords of his sins. He shall die without instruction; and in the greatness of his folly he shall go astray (Proverbs 5:20-23).

Deuteronomy 5:18: Neither shalt thou commit adultery (which stretches to all forms of immorality).

My son, keep thy father's commandment, and forsake not the law of thy mother: Bind them continually upon thine heart, and tie them about thy neck. When thou goest, it shall lead thee; when thou sleepest, it shall keep thee; and when thou awakest, it shall talk with thee (Proverbs 6:20-22).

You can see the evil that is warned in the last part of this chapter, verses 23-35. We want to let the Word of God protect the heart and adorn the neck. This is so we can see the outward beauty of a holy life, and inward wealth of general truths.

Leviticus 20:10 states: And the man that committeth adultery with another man's wife, even he that committeth adultery with his neighbour's wife, the adulterer and the adulteress shall surely be put to death.

To keep you from the evil woman, from the flattery of the tongue of a strange woman. Lust not after her beauty in thine heart; neither let her take thee with her eyelids. For by means of a whorish woman a man is brought to a piece of bread: and the adulteress will hunt for the precious life, Can a man take fire in his bosom, and his clothes not be burned? Can one go upon hot coals, and his feet not burned? So he that goeth into his neighbor's wife; whosoever toucheth her shall not be innocent, Men do not despise a thief, if he steal to satisfy his soul when he is hungry; But if he be found, he shall restore sevenfold; he shall give all the substance of his house. But whoso committeth adultery with a woman lacketh understanding: he that doeth it destroyeth his own soul. A wound and dishonor shall he get; and his reproach shall not be wiped away. For jealousy is the rage of a man: therefore he will not spare in the day of vengeance. He will not regard any ransom: neither will he rest content, though thou givest many gifts. (Proverbs 6:24-35).

As sanctified believers, you should not have the spirit of concealment or disguise:

The eyes of the adulterer waiteth for the twilight, saying, no eye shall see me: and disguiseth his face (Job 24:15).

Job didn't have to pretend that he had chastity; he made a solemn declaration of his integrity:

I made a covenant with my eyes; why then should I think upon a maid? (Job 31:1)

Because strait is the gate, and narrow is the way, which leadeth unto life, and few there be that find it (Matthew 7:14).

But he who misses me or sins against me wrongs and injures himself; all who hate me love and court death (Proverbs 8:36 AMP).

But whoever commits adultery with a woman lacks heart and understanding (moral principle and prudence); he who does it is destroying his own life (Proverbs 6:32 AMP).

> *But I say to you that everyone who so much as looks at a woman with evil desire for her has already committed adultery with her in his heart (Matthew 5:28 AMP).*

It was made clear by Jesus' teachings on adultery it is not going after the outward appearance but inward change. He doesn't want religious zeal, but transformed men and women. He wants people who are set apart for Him, and love to do His will. Most of the world is captured by this "strange woman" and do not realize that sin is destructive. Just a small number of people are following the right way of the scriptures. If one continues in adultery and refuses to repent, it will bring spiritual death. One will experience spiritual death (which is being separated from God because of sin), if we do not ask God's forgiveness and cleansing from sin.

> *BEHOLD, the Lord's hand is not shortened, that it cannot save; neither his ear heavy, that it cannot hear: But your iniquities have separated between you and your God, and your sins have hid his face from you, that he will not hear (Isaiah 59:1-2).*

> *If we confess our sins, he is faithful and just to forgive us our sins, and to cleanse us from all unrighteousness (1 John 1:9).*

We can see the consequences of physical adultery in these scriptures, but they also tell of the truth of spiritual adultery by forsaking Christ (see Romans 1-4). Joseph's brethren also displayed jealousy in Genesis 37:4:

> *And when his brethren saw that their father loved him more than all his brethren, they hated him, and could not speak peaceably unto him.*

We can also see the ever presence of God the Father's instruction, divine teaching, and His work:

O God, thou hast taught me from my youth: and hitherto have I declared thy wondrous works. [guidance and divine counsel] (Psalm 71:17).

For this God is our God for ever and ever: he will be our guide even unto death (Psalm 48:14).

God the Son watches over our lives with infinite care:

Behold, he that keepeth Is'ra-el shall neither slumber nor sleep (Psalm 121:4).

Casting the whole of your care [all your anxieties, all your worries, all your concerns, once and for all] on Him, for He cares for you affectionately and cares about you watchfully (1 Peter 5:7 AMP).

Cast your burden on the Lord [releasing the weight of it] and He will sustain you; He will never allow the [consistently] righteous to be moved (made to slip, fall, or fail) (Psalm 55:22 AMP).

For the commandment is a lamp; the law is light; and reproofs of instruction are the way of life. The Word is a light. Thy word is a lamp unto my feet, and a light unto my path (Proverbs 6:23; Psalm 119:105).

We live in an evil world so this is why we need to apply God's Word and let the Word shine on our problems so we will not stumble in blackness.

We can see in these verses that we can turn away from

Christ and accept another gospel:

> *I am surprised and astonished that you are so quickly turning renegade and deserting Him Who invited and called you by the grace (unmerited favor) of Christ (the Messiah) [and that you are transferring your allegiance] to a different [even an opposition] gospel (Galatians 1:6 AMP).*

> *For if he that cometh preacheth another Jesus, whom we have not preached, or If ye receive another spirit, which ye have not received, or another gospel, which ye have not accepted, ye might well bear with him (2 Corinthians 11:4; see also Romans 7:1-4).*

Importance of Prayer

Dr. Estella Boyd sacrificed her life in fasting and praying for her daughters and sons and the people of God. God not only gave her a vision about leaders, but a real burden for them, the work of the Lord, and that they are delivered.

> *The burden which Habakkuk the prophet did see (Habakkuk 1:1)*

Habakkuk was deeply troubled with the injustice that prevailed in his land and was desirous that the Lord would act against it. In the first four verses of this book, the prophet cries out for God to answer his question. He begs God to respond to the injustice, the violence, and the perversion of the nation.

> *A PRAYER of Habakkuk the prophet upon Shigionoth. (The word Shigionoth is the plural of Shiggaion, and means a crying aloud) O Lord, I have heard thy speech, and was*

afraid: O Lord, revive thy work in the midst of the years, in the midst of years, make known; in wrath remember mercy. God came from Teman, and the Holy One from mount Paran. Selah. His glory covered the heavens, and the earth was full of his praise. And his brightness was as the light; he had horns coming out of his hand: and there was the hiding of his power (Habakkuk 3:1-4).

The same burden that God gave to Habakkuk was given to Mother Boyd: to see the glory of God and His praise in God's Church. She could not stop praying for God's leaders and His church until the people were walking in the will of God and the presence of God was upon them. She was given the gift of the laying on of hands to impart into God's people.

> *For I long to see you, that I may impart unto you some spiritual gift, to the end ye may be established; (Romans 1:11)*

The glory of God would fill the temple and God would be in the midst of the people, bringing mass deliverance, healing and salvation. They didn't have to make an altar call in her services, the people would come up and ask to be saved. She would call me and ask me to touch and agree with her in praying for many leaders.

> *Verily I say unto you, Whatsoever ye shall bind on earth shall be bound in heaven: and whatsoever ye shall loose on earth shall be loosed in heaven. Again I say unto you, That if two of you shall agree on earth as touching any thing that they shall ask, it shall be done for them of my Father which is in heaven (Matthew 18:18-19).*

She taught me to give myself to prayer and to the ministry of the Word, (see Acts 6:4) then the prayer would be honored and ratified in Heaven. Mother Boyd would always say every Word of God's is loaded. The set apart ones for God know what Romans 8:26 AMP says:

> *So too the [Holy] Spirit comes to our aid and bears us up in our weakness; for we do not know what prayer to offer nor how to offer it worthily as we ought, but the Spirit Himself goes to meet our supplication and pleads in our behalf with unspeakable yearnings and groanings too deep for utterance,*

This kind of intercession comes from the Holy Spirit and from suffering to glory, brings divine help and the work of the Holy Spirit.

Paul Describes the Spirit-Filled Life

There is a difference between Christian mentoring and the world's mentoring. Christian mentors do not build a reliance on themselves, but point their protégés to God. The life Paul navigates is of liberty (Romans 8:1-8), hope (8:9-15), and power (8:26-30). Observe how the Holy Spirit navigates life for us (The Maxwell Leadership Bible):

He intercedes and groans for us (Romans 8:22, 23, 26 and 27):

1. He directs and testifies to us (John 16:13; Acts 20:22,23; Romans 8:14)
2. He empowers and anoints us for service (Acts 1:8; Romans 8:28-37; 1 John 2:27)
3. He searches and enables us to discern (Romans 8:26,27; 1 Corinthians 2:9-15)
4. He confirms and bears witness with us (Romans 8:14-16; 1 John 5:5-9).

Mother Boyd would have me to search out many scriptures to pray and ward off evil around leaders. Apostle Paul said "pray for us."

> *Paul craveth for the set apart ones prayers…and be glorified (extolled) and triumph, bring forth its full power and positive effect in people's lives), even as [it has done] with you, And that we may be delivered from perverse (improper, unrighteous) and wicked (actively malicious) men, for not everybody has faith and is held by it. Yet the Lord is faithful, and He will strengthen [you] and set you on a firm foundation and guard you from the evil [one] (2 Thessalonians 3:1-3 AMP).*

When the Word of God has free course, God can accomplish its intended purpose.

Abstain From Evil

Abstain means: *to keep oneself back; refrain voluntarily*. The Greek word *apechomai* (ap-ekh'-om-ahee) means *to hold oneself off, abstaining from evil practices, moral and ceremonial*. God wants us to shun evil:

> *Abstain from evil [shrink from it and keep aloof from it] in whatever form or whatever kind it may be (1 Thessalonians 5:22 AMP).*

> *Let him eschew evil, and do good; let him seek peace, and ensue it (1 Peter 3:11)*

> *Now these things were our examples, to the intent we should not lust after evil things, as they also lusted (1 Corinthians 10:6).*

This means evil desires and idolatry are forbidden for us; so shun evil.

Let love be without dissimulation. Abhor that which is evil; cleave to that which is good. And oppress not the widow, nor the fatherless, the stranger, nor the poor; and let none of you imagine evil against his brother in your heart (Romans 12:9, Zechariah 7:10).

A wise man feareth, and departeth from evil: but the fool rageth, and is confident (Proverbs 14:16).

Turn not to the right hand nor to the left: remove thy foot from evil. When you love the Lord, and hate evil: he preseserveth the souls of his saints; he delivereth them out of the hand of the wicked. Depart from evil, and do good; seek peace, and pursue it.

Reverential Fear of God

The reverential fear of God is missing from the Christian and it ought not to be.

And unto man he said, Behold, the fear of the Lord, that is wisdom; and to depart from evil is understanding (Job 28:28).

And now, Israel, what doth the Lord thy God require of thee, but to fear the Lord thy God, to walk in all his ways, and to love him, and to serve the Lord thy God with all thy heart and with all thy soul (Deuteronomy 10:12).

You shall walk after the Lord your God, which means be a follower, keep his commandments fear God only, be obedient, and serve God.

That all the people of the earth might know the hand of the Lord, that it is mighty: that ye might fear the Lord your God for ever (Joshua 4:24).

Now therefore, [reverently] fear the Lord and serve Him in sincerity and in truth; put away the gods which your fathers served on the other side of the [Euphrates] River and in Egypt, and serve the Lord (Joshua 24:14 AMP, see 1 Chronicles 16:30, 2 Chronicles 19:17).

Be not wise in thine on own eyes: fear the Lord, and depart from evil (Proverbs 3:7).

Let us hear the conclusion of the whole matter: Fear God, and keep his commandment: for this is the whole duty of man (Ecclesiastes 12:13).

Sanctify the Lord of hosts himself; and let him be your fear, and let him be your dread (Isaiah 8:13).

And fear not them which kill the body, but are not able to kill the soul: but rather fear him which is able to destroy both soul and body in hell (Matthew 10:28; see also 1 Peter 1:17, 2:17).

Sanctification

Dr. Boyd would teach us that sanctification process involves the whole man. There is no reason to waste prayer about whether it is God's will to get involved sexually with anyone who is not our spouse; the Holy Spirit is always grieved when sexual intercourse is outside of marriage.

For this is the will of God, that you should be consecrated (separated and set apart for pure and holy living): that you should abstain and shrink from all sexual vice. That each one of you should know how to possess (control, manage) his own body in consecration (purity, separated from things profane) and honor, (see 1 Corinthians 3:16) Not [to be used] in the passion of lust like the heathen, who are ignorant of the true God and have no knowledge of His will. That no man transgress and overreach his brother and defraud him in this matter or defraud his brother in business. For the Lord is an avenger in all these things, as we have already warned you solemnly and told you plainly. For God has not called us to impurity but to consecration [to dedicate ourselves to the most thorough purity]. Therefore whoever disregards (sets aside and rejects this) disregards not man but God, Whose [very] Spirit [Whom] He gives to you is holy (chaste, pure) (1 Thessalonians 4:3-8 AMP).

The believers who abstain from certain evils live before the world. We have to remind ourselves that this world is not our home, just remember we are aliens and strangers here.

Dearly beloved, I beseech you as strangers and pilgrims, abstain from fleshly lusts, (the evil desires, the passions of the flesh, your lower nature) which war against the soul; (1 Peter 2:11).

Abstain from evil [shrink from it keep aloof from it] in whatever form or whatever kind it may be. And may the God of peace Himself sanctify you through and through [separate you from profane things, make you pure and wholly consecrated to God]; and may your spirit and soul and body be preserved sound and complete [and found] blameless at the coming of our Lord Jesus Christ (the Messiah) (1 Thessalonians 5:22-24 AMP).

Chapter 5

Sanctification Gives Us Authority

Sanctification gives us the right to command and enforce personal influence. *Authority* means: *The right to command and to enforce obedience; the right to act, decide, delegated right or power, those having the power to govern or command, power.* The Greek word for *authority* is *exousia* (ex-oo-see'-ah) means: *In the sense of ability, privilege, force, capacity, competency, freedom, delegated influence.*

Dr. Estella Boyd lived a sanctified life and God delegated authority to her for accepting a set apart life. Many times when I would travel with her as a nurse, I would ask questions about how she stayed anointed and sometimes we would go over the scriptures in the *Daughter of Zion Handbook*. Sanctification was the first group of scriptures. I said to her "Mother, this is a whole lot" and she told me, "let God begin the process." I obeyed and started to study sanctification and asked God to sanctify me like her, so I could stay anointed. She also told me everything God puts His finger on in my life, everything that He wanted me to give up, to obey. I began to surrender all to God, not my will but Thine will be done in my life (see Matthew 26:39).

I began to study sanctification in depth until God begin to put it in me. In studying sanctification in depth, God showed me that sanctification gives us authority and I saw this in Mother Boyd's life. She would pray the prayer of authority for her sons and daughters for God to sanctify them and that they would be fruitful. Another group of scriptures we studied out of the *Daughter of Zion Handbook* was supplication, prayer of praise, and the prayer of thanksgiving. Mother Boyd taught me the prayer of authority, which means we declared or proclaimed our prayer. One of the *Daughter of Zion Handbook*'s creeds she taught us was: "We believe that watchfulness, prayer, fasting and wailing is the only method by which we can get our petition answered from God." If you intend to pray with authority, pray the prayer of binding and loosing in Matthew 18:18. Mother knew that earth does not pray, it bind and loose. She taught me different types of prayer.

Jesus Prayed for His Disciples

> *John 17:5-19 And now, O Father, glorify thou me with thine own self with the glory which I had with thee before the world was. I have manifested thy name unto the men which thou gavest me out of the world: thine they were, and thou gavest them me; and they have kept thy word. Now they have known that all things whatsoever thou hast given me are of thee. For I have given unto them the words which thou gavest me; and they have received them, and have known surely that I came out from thee, and they have believed that thou didst send me. I pray for them; I pray not for the world, but for them which thou hast given me; for they are thine. And all mine are thine, and thine are mine; and I am glorified in them. And now I am no more in the world, but these are in the world, and I come to thee. Holy Father, keep thou thine own name those whom thou hast given me, that they may be one, as we are. While I was with them in the world, I kept them in thy name: those that thou gavest me I have kept, and none of them is lost, but the son of perdition: that the Scripture might be fulfilled. And now*

come I to thee; and these things I speak in the world, that they might have my joy fulfilled in themselves. I have given them thy word; and the world hath hated them, because they are not of the world, even as I am not of the world. I pray not that thou shouldest take them out of the world, but that thou shouldest keep them from evil. They are not of the world, even as I am not of the world. Sanctify them through thy truth: thy word is truth. As thou hast sent me into the world, even so have I also sent them into the world. And for their sakes I sanctify myself, that they also might be sanctified through the truth.

Dr. Boyd would pray that the leaders in authority would sanctify themselves. Also, that they would be able to win in spiritual warfare (see Ephesians 6:12-18). This kind of prayer is different from the common everyday prayer. We know that the Church's spiritual authority is based on spirituality. So we should humble ourselves before God, and obey him. We can bring out one more point: the one who is to be in authority must be sanctified from the public. Even though Jesus was sent of God and faithfully communed with God, Jesus still broadcasted, for his disciples' sakes, "I sanctify Myself."

When Jesus Sanctified Himself

When Jesus sanctified Himself, for the cause of His disciples, Jesus abstained from doing numerous of things which were best lawful to him. Apostle Paul, in Philippians 2:3-9 AMP, wrote about the example of Christ's humility is set before the Philippians as an example to follow. Paul reminded them of Christ's incarnation also.

V. 3. We see that our Lord and Saviour Jesus Christ motives for what He did were set apart for God.

V. 4. Also Jesus interest and unselfishness were set apart for God.

V. 5. Jesus attitude was set apart for God and His purpose was set apart and His mind was set apart for God. (John 8:29 Jesus always did the things that please God).

V. 6. Jesus character was set apart because He gave up his divine form.

V. 7. Jesus was set apart and emptied Himself apart to be a servant for God. He became as a man.

V. 8. Jesus set Himself apart through obedience to serve God no matter what the cost.

V. 9. Jesus was given authority above all because He set Himself apart for God.

In 1 Thessalonians 5:22,23 AMP, the Apostle Paul wrote to the church at Thessalonica:

to abstain from evil [shrink from and it and keep aloof from it] in whatever form or whatever kind it may be. And may the God of peace Himself sanctify you [separate you from profane things, make you pure and wholly consecrated to God]; and may your spirit and soul and body be preserved sound and complete [and found] blameless at the coming of our Lord Jesus Christ (the Messiah).

The Apostles were eyewitnesses of the authority Jesus walked in because they observed his life. Jesus suffered unjustly and endured it without complaint and found no guile on his lips. They saw that even his attitude was set apart for God when He was threatened or attacked.

He was guilty of no sin, neither was deceit (guile) ever found on His lips. [Isaiah 53:9]. When he was reviled and insulted, He did not revile or offer insult in return; [when] He was abused and suffered, He was made no threats [of vengeance]; but He trusted [Himself and everything] to Him Who judges fairly (1 Peter 2:22,23).

Sanctification frees you so that you can walk in authority as Jesus did. Jesus ruled over his own spirit that is why in any city He went in, He had authority (see Proverbs 16:32). Since He was most holy, we need to humble ourselves. Jesus never walked proud.

But He gives us more and more grace (power of the Holy Spirit, to meet this evil tendency and all others fully). That is why He says, God sets Himself against the proud and haughty, but gives grace [continually] to the lowly (those who are humble enough to receive it) [Proverbs 3:34] So be subject to God. Resist the devil [stand firm against him], and he will flee from you (James 4:6-7 AMP).

When we allow God to set us apart, we will not cast away our confidence. We will see clearly that we have need of patience that, after we have done the will of God. (See Hebrews 10:35,36). Then we will be able to allow God to sanctify our anger without sinning and be holy, because our God is holy. *But as the One Who called you is holy, you yourselves also be holy in all your conduct and manner of living. For it is written, You shall be holy, for I am holy* (1 Peter 1:15,16 AMP). This holiness will cause us to be sanctified from the world. It is also why Jesus sanctified himself for our sake and we will be able to accept persecution accordingly (see Matthew 5:43-45). Holiness will help us to have self-control; Jesus knew how valuable God's authority was to Him, that is why he did the things the Father said. Therefore, He could unveil to us that we can be separate from the world (see John 2:15,16 AMP). Jesus wants us to have a clear understanding of why He sanctified Himself.

Lonely in Authority

When I began to accept the process of God's sanctification in my life, it taught me that He will sanctify you and set you apart from others. I'm from a large family, six sisters and now two brothers, when you are used to being around a lot of people, I still felt alone. Jesus knows how to comfort you through His word, (Matthew 28:20) Lo, I am with you always, even unto the end of the world. Amen. There will be times when we fellowship with our brothers and sisters occasionally. But when we are set apart for God, you know that authority belongs to God, so pride has nothing to do with God's authority. It is an honor when God allows us to operate in His authority and this is why we need to pursue sanctification:

> *And that ye may put difference between holy and unholy, and between unclean and clean; (Leviticus 10:10).*

When you are sanctified you will be different from others; our conversion must be holy, (see 1 Peter 1:15,16). You may not be able to do even some legitimate things and you cannot even speak many lawful words. Jesus only said and did what the Father told him. You know that it is not an outward make up; we as leaders must pursue holiness and the only way to attain it is to embrace the model Christ gives. Since God is holy we must copy what we see Him do. This is the only way we can be God's delegated authority. We as leaders in authority must represent God in our conversation and conduct.

Moses and Aaron Sin

> *And the Lord said to Moses and Aaron, Because you did not believe in (rely on, cling to) Me to sanctify Me in the eyes of*

the Israelites, you therefore shall not bring this congregation into the land which I have given them (Numbers 20:12 AMP).

For there is no respect of persons with God, (Romans 2:11) with him one man is not different from another. Obeying God always brings blessing and disobedience brings penalty. Moses allowed his anger and frustration to bring out the motive of his flesh (see Psalm 106:32-33). So if we do not allow God to set us apart in a higher level we will be unfit to be in authority. When you are in authority, it requires you to be level headed and you must be sanctified yourselves. God's set apart ones cannot go where others may. It is imperative that we obey the Lord. …Behold, to obey is better than sacrifice, and to hearken than the fat of rams (1 Samuel 15:22). Because your service will be tested, God places a high value on obedience. If we are not set apart, our heart reveals its true nature. Our obedience toward God will help us commit ourselves to obey what God commands us to do.

In Leviticus 9, Moses and Aaron are performing their priestly duties and the glory of God comes down. The fire of God consumes their sacrifices upon the altar. Aaron's sons in Leviticus 10 did not follow their father's example. They did things their own way, and God judged them by sending fire down to consume them, as servants of God, we must keep our affection on things above. There is a price to pay to walk in authority. Also in Leviticus 10, Aaron's sons did not obey God's command to abstain from strong drink. There are things as servants of God that we cannot participate in. There is a price to pay to walk in God's will and authority, as we serve God we are called to a higher standard than others. Some people may do certain things, but for those who will walk in authority, it costs much more. For whom much is given much shall be required. God has a standard of His word that he will not change for anyone. If we desire to walk in God's authority we must also be willing to pay the price, so start the process of pursuing sanctification.

Even if we do not fully understand those commands, what we do know is obedience is better than sacrifice. To be in authority requires restraint; we must sanctify ourselves. Stick with obeying the Spirit of the Lord as He teaches within you. We may feel lonely sometimes and miss being with others, nevertheless this is the price of authority when we are set apart for God. *Because the carnal mind is enmity against God: for it is not subject to the law of God, neither indeed can be* (Romans 8:7).

If we do not pursue sanctification like our Lord, we are not qualified to be in authority. When walking in authority it is perfectly normal to maintain fellowship with one another. *But if we walk in the light, as he is in the light, we have fellowship one with another, and the blood of Jesus Christ his Son cleanseth us from all sin* (1 John 1:7). As representatives of God, we must pursue sanctification so we can be examples to all. These things command and teach. Let no man despise thy youth; but be thou an example of the believers, in word, in conversation, in charity, in spirit, in faith, in purity (1 Tim.4:11,12). Continue serving with all the brethren, never putting anyone in false placement of being in a special class.

Set Apart Affections

Colossians 1:27 AMP says:

To whom God was pleased to make known how great for the

Gentiles are the riches of the glory of this mystery, which is Christ within and among you, the Hope of [realizing the] glory.

It is important for us to be presented spotless, (2 Peter 3:14) and faultless (Jude 24) in unutterable glory. In Old Testament times, the Holy Spirit came upon chosen men women of God to enable them to accomplish God's will--but no one ever imagined that God would actually take residence in believers, as He does today.

Mother Boyd would say to whom God would make known to His saints what are the riches of His glory. When you walk in authority, you will be rooted in Him, and built up in Him. (Colossians 2:6-10 AMP):

As you have therefore received Christ, [even] Jesus the Lord, [so] walk (regulate your lives and conduct yourselves) in union with and conformity to Him. Have the roots [of your being] firmly and deeply planted [in Him, fixed and founded in Him], being continually built up in Him, becoming increasingly more confirmed and established in the faith, just as you were taught, and abounding and overflowing in it with thanksgiving. See to it that no one carries you off as spoil or makes you yourselves captive by his so-called philosophy and intellectualism and vain deceit (idle fancies and plain nonsense), following human tradition (men's ideas of material rather than the spiritual world), just crude notions following the rudimentary and elemental teachings of the universe and disregarding [the teachings of] Christ (the Messiah). For in Him the whole fullness of Deity (the Godhead) continues to dwell in bodily form [giving complete expression of the divine nature]. And you are in Him, made full and having come to fullness of life [in Christ you too are filled with the Godhead-Father, Son and Holy Spirit-and reach full spiritual stature]. And He is the Head of all rule and authority [of every angelic principality and power].

This is how you receive salvation through faith, and grow into maturity; your faith should be depending upon God to make you into the image of Christ.

Once you walk in authority, you will focus on your position in Christ. We can renew our thought life and focus our mind on things above.

IF THEN you have been raised with Christ [to a new life, thus sharing His resurrection from the dead], aim at and seek the [rich, eternal treasures] that are above, where Christ is, seated at the right hand of God. And set your minds and keep them set on what is above (the higher things), not on the things that are on the earth (Colossians 3:1-2 AMP).

Be not conformed to this world: but be ye transformed by the renewing of mind, that ye may prove what is that good, and acceptable, and perfect, will of God. (Romans 12:2).

Mother Boyd would say sanctification will bring a new internal standard and you will know your old life is dead (Colossians 3:3-7). She would share things with us that you do not hear today like not to return back to the things God delivered us from and do not go back to past habits. We have to be about the business of the kingdom just as our Lord and Savior Jesus Christ.

But Jesus said to him, Allow the dead to bury their own dead; but as for you, go and publish abroad throughout all regions the kingdom of God. Another also said, I will follow You, Lord, and become Your disciple and side with Your party; but let me first say good-bye to those at my home.

SANCTIFICATION GIVES US AUTHORITY

Jesus said to him, No one who puts his hand to the plow and looks back [to the things behind] is fit for the kingdom of God (Luke 9:60-62).

This was letting the disciples know they cannot serve Him if they look back or do anything that is not for His purpose in God's kingdom. Keeping one's affection on things above allows God's servants to walk in His authority. When we disobey God, we cannot walk in God's authority.

God will anoint his delegated authority to serve and praise Him for seeing His glory. God's delegated authority will be disciples so they will be able to distinguish between the holy and unholy or might I say the unclean and the clean. When fellowship with one another we should be able to discern from being close to God how we should not be careless. The priests who serve God in Leviticus 21 were commanded to sanctify themselves. Mother Boyd would teach us that God commands us not to defile ourselves. Another one of The *Daughter of Zion Handbook* creeds she told us was: "We, believe that as daughters, we must keep ourselves pure and virtuous from the defilement of the world." Mother was sanctified in clothing and body. God gave her the gift of laying on of hands. When God gave her to lay hands, she wore handkerchiefs and towels; it would bring mass deliverance as Paul did in Acts 19:6-12. She walked in authority as God anointed His handmaid.

Marriage: Christ and the Church

Mother told me when I get married God will sanctify my marriage and He did just that. Everything she shared with me is coming to pass. I'm still praising and giving God glory for our saved and sanctified marriage. So for the high priest, the demands of God were more. I believe the higher the office, the stricter the demand. God is concerned with whether or not His servants have sanctified themselves.

> *Wives, be subject (be submissive and adapt yourselves) to your own husbands as [a service] to the Lord. For the husband is head of the wife as Christ is the Head of the church, Himself the Savior of [His] body. As the church is subject to Christ, so let wives also be subject in everything to their husbands. Husbands, love your wives, as Christ loved the church and gave Himself up for her, So that He might sanctify her, having cleansed her by the washing of water with the Word, Even so husbands should love their wives as [being in a sense] their own bodies. He who loves his own wife loves himself. However, let each man of you [without exception] love his wife as [being in a sense] his very own self; and let the wife see that she respects and reverences her husband [that she notices him, regards him, honors him, prefers him, venerates, and esteems him; and that she defers to him, praises him, and loves and admires him exceedingly] (Ephesians 5:22-26,28,33 AMP)*

See Also:

- Colossians 3:18: Godly fear, Wives' Duty
- 1 Timothy 2:11: Woman's Home Duties
- 1 Peter 3:7; Colossians 1:24: Husband's Duty, Christ's Love, Church Precious
- 2 Timothy 2:21: Sanctification
- 1 Peter 1:19: Unblemished
- Colossians 3:19: Conjugal Love
- 1 Peter 3:7: Marriage Sacred

Paul wants the same attitude toward our relationship with each other (which is really submission). He calls on the husband to be Christ-representation or likeness

(Ephesians 5:21). We must be subject to one another out of reverence for Christ (the Messiah, the Anointed One). (Ephesians 5:23-25). Christ is our greatest example of leading the church. He sanctified Himself. He died on a cross, provided, taught, wept, and healed. When you walk in authority you give up yourself for someone else. This is taking responsibility pertaining to developing your relationship (Ephesians 5:25).

Mother Estella Boyd had this creed as part of the *Daughter of Zion Handbook*: We, believe that as mothers we must not provoke our children to wrath, but train and draw them to Christ with loving kindness. I obey this creed and my son Fred Abernathy is saved today. Here are some scriptures that I searched out to pray and instruct for my son. (Colossians1:9-14 I would pray continually and Deuteronomy 4:9,6:11,31:13; Psalm 78:5; Proverbs 22:6,28:9 and John 21:15)

> *CHILDREN, OBEY your parents in the Lord [as His representatives], for this is just and right. Fathers, do not irritate and provoke your children to anger [do not exasperate them to resentment], but rear them [tenderly] in the training and discipline and the counsel and admonition of the Lord. You masters, act on the same [principle] toward them and give up threatening and using violent and abusive words, knowing that He Who is both their Master and yours is in heaven, and that there is no respect of persons (no partiality) with Him (Ephesians 6:1,4,9 AMP).*

Whatever we do, God is exalted and He is the judge.

> *GOD STANDS in the assembly [of the representatives] of God; in the midst of the magistrates or judges He gives judgment [as] among the gods. How long will you [magistrates*

or judges] judge unjustly and show partiality to the wicked? Selah [pause, and calmly think of that]! (Psalm 82:1,2 AMP)

Husbands and Wives' Qualification as Ministers

Paul brings out some of the same things he shared with Timothy, one of the main traits had to do with personal character, not gifts or skills. What was most important to Paul was a blameless personal life:

> [These elders should be] men who are of unquestionable integrity and are irreproachable, the husband of [but] one wife, whose children are [well trained and are] believers, not open to the accusation of being loose in morals and conduct or unruly and disorderly. For the bishop (an overseer) as God's steward must be blameless, not self-willed or arrogant or presumptuous; he must not be quick-tempered or given to drink or pugnacious (brawling, violent); he must not be grasping and greedy for filthy lucre (financial gain); But he must be hospitable (loving and a friend to believers, especially to strangers and foreigners); [he must be] a lover of goodness [of good people and good things], sober-minded (sensible, discreet), upright and fair-minded, a devout man and religiously correct, temperate and keeping himself in hand (Titus 1:6-8 AMP).

Family life:

> He must rule his own household well, keeping his children under control, with true dignity, commanding their respect in every way and keeping them respectful, For if a man does not know how to rule his own household, how is he to take care of the church of God? He must not be a new convert, or he may [develop a beclouded and stupid state of mind] as

the result of pride [be blinded by conceit, and] fall into the condemnation that the devil [once] did (1 Timothy 3:4-6 AMP).

Social life:

Tell [them all] these things, Urge (advise, encourage, warn) and rebuke with full authority. Let no one despise or disregard or think little of you [conduct yourself and your teaching so as to command respect] (Titus 2:15 AMP).

Professional life:

Let no one despise or think less of you because of your youth, but be an example (pattern) for the believers in speech, in conduct, in love, in faith, and in purity (1 Timothy 4:12 AMP).

For even to this were you called [it is inseparable from your vocation]. For Christ also suffered for you, leaving you [His personal] example, so that you should follow in His footsteps (1 Peter 2:21 AMP).

The husband and the wife have God-given authority. To maintain order, everyone must do their part. As parents, one must communicate to one's children. The husband must communicate with his wife. In the church, the elders must communicate with God's people. God's authority must be maintained by His people. Authority is evidence of sanctification. Representing God is to represent authority; pursuing sanctification will help you walk in authority and be an example to all.

Essential Sanctification

When you walk in authority, you will know the fundamentals of sanctification. So if you are without sanctification, there is no authority. When set apart for God, you will not live with groups and be in authority. Mother Boyd would tell us that you cannot walk in authority, when you have a carnal mind (Romans 8:5-8). The more God uses you, the more He will separate you. The Bible says in Romans 13:1 AMP:

> *Let every person be loyally subject to the governing (civil) authorities. For there is no authority except from God [by His permission, His sanction], and those that exist do so by God's appointment.*

See also Proverbs 8:15; Daniel 2:21; 4:35. Let us allow God to sanctify us from everything unclean or unholy.

Jesus could have done whatever He liked, but He chose to sanctify Himself for the sake of his disciples. Mother Boyd kept a high standard in holiness until she went on to be with the Father. As sons and daughters, let us desire to please God, and allow Him to do a deeper sanctification in us. Sanctification will set you apart from the common. This does not mean that we are holier than anyone else. We know all authority belongs to God and He will help us to walk in authority. This is why it is so important that we live by example and not fail people who we have are under our authority. How can obedience be continued if we do not operate in this kind of authority? The church would be in chaos.

The one in authority will serve God and has counted the cost. That person will not try to take the glory, but keep pressing to that high calling in Christ Jesus. *I press on toward the goal to win the [supreme and heavenly] prize to which*

God in Christ Jesus is calling us upward (Philippians 3:14 AMP). Jesus is calling us to come up and we will not worry about being alone, but being sanctified. Let us surrender all so we can believe God's authority will be restored back to His church.

I believe this scripture reflects what Mother Boyd would say about the church in its first glory:

> *Who is left among you who saw this house in its former glory? And how do you see it now? Is not this in your sight as nothing in comparison to that? (Haggai 2:3 AMP)* Read what God said He wants to be in His house in (2 Samuel 7:13; 1 Kings 5:5).

From even the beginning of the Bible, God showed Adam and Eve that to walk in authority they had to be separated from the tree of the knowledge of good and evil (Genesis 2:15-17). This is a great example of why we should pursue sanctification in our lives as believers, as well as leaders that would walk in authority. We have to do this so that the enemy will not have exercise victory over us. The Bible tells us in 1 John 5:4: *For whatever is born of God is victorious over the world; and this is the victory that conquers the world, even our faith.* God wants us to walk in authority on earth today, but it will require us being set apart for Him.

Chapter 6

Doing the Will of God

Pursuing sanctification will help you establish a divine relationship with God. Jesus says in Matthew 12:50 AMP: *For whoever does the will of my father in heaven the same is my brother, and sister, and mother.* Jesus came to earth to do the will of His Father, and so anyone who has the same goal is one in spirit with him. A genuine desire to please God creates a stronger bond than anything else in the world. [The Life Principles Bible]

The Greek word for *will* in Matthew 12:50 is *thelema*, thel'-ay-mah: It means *a determination, choice, purpose or decree. What one wishes or has determined shall be done.* God has a choice, purpose, decree and a determination for everyone. Jesus is also saying you who will enter into the kingdom of heaven will be a doer of the will of God. Matthew 7:21 says:

> *Not everyone that saith unto me, Lord, Lord, shall enter into the kingdom of heaven; but he that doeth the will of my father which is in heaven. Jesus will show you the ones who are set apart for God.*
>
> *Why do you call ye Me, Lord, Lord, and do not [practice] what I tell you? For everyone who comes to Me and listens to My words [in order to heed their teaching] and does them, I will show you what he is like: He is like a man building a house, who dug and went down deep and laid a foundation*

> upon the rock; and when a flood arose, the torrent broke against that house and could not shake or move it, because it bad been securely built or founded on a rock. But he who merely hears and does not practice doing My words is like a man who built a house on the ground without a foundation, against which the torrent burst, and immediately it collapsed and fell, and the breaking and ruin of that house was great (Luke 6:46-49 AMP).

> John 13:17 AMP If ye know these things, blessed and happy and to be envied are you if you practice them [if you act accordingly and really do them].

Jesus does not just want those to know His will but those who will do also, and faith in God will help you do His will. When you are set apart for God you will know how to obey the law. For not the hearers of the law are just before God, but the doers of the law shall be justified (Romans 2:13).

Doers Not Hearers Only

> But be doers of the Word [obey the message], and not merely listeners to it, betraying yourselves [into deception by reasoning contrary to the Truth] (James 1:22 AMP).

Pursuing sanctification will help you carry out God's purpose forever.

> And the world passes away and disappears, and with it the forbidden cravings (the passionate desires, the lust) of it; but he who does the will of God and carries out His purposes in his life abides (remains) forever (1 John 2:17 AMP).

> Blessed are they that do his commandments, that they may have right to the tree of life, and may enter in through the

gates into the city (Revelations 22:14).

Being a doer by obeying and keeping his commandments brings great blessings.

The Law in the Heart

Submission to the divine will gives results of the inward law. *I delight to do Your will, O my God; yes, Your law is within my heart* (Psalm 40:8 AMP). When you accept the process of God sanctifying you, it will be a joy in serving God. *Serve the Lord with gladness! Come before His presence with singing* (Psalm 100:2). God does not want us to do His will reluctantly, but delight in doing what pleases Him. When we have the law of God in our hearts, we will learn how to live in the midst of the wicked as David said in Psalm 37. The sanctified ones accept the law of God in their hearts and learn to do the will of God because of their reverential fear of Him.

> *But this is the covenant which I will make with the house of Israel: After those days, says the Lord, I will put my law within them, and on their hearts will I write it, and I will be their God, and they will be my people (Jeremiah 31:33 AMP).*

> *And I will make an everlasting covenant with them: I will not turn away from following them to do them good, and I will put My [reverential] fear in their hearts, so that they will not depart from Me (Jeremiah 32:40 AMP).*

> *They show that the essential requirements of the Law are written in their hearts and are operating there, with which their consciences (sense of right and wrong) also bear witness: and their [moral] decisions (their arguments of reason,*

their condemning or approving thoughts) will accuse or perhaps defend and excuse [them] (Romans 2:15 AMP).

Apostle Paul identifies with the peoples inward struggles with sinful desires and the downward tendency in Romans 7:14-25. When you do the will of God in your heart, you will not try to find excuses, because you totally depend upon the Holy Spirit. Christ had a more excellent ministry.

But as it now is, He [Christ] has acquired a [priestly] ministry which is as much superior and more excellent [than the old] as the covenant (the agreement) of which He is the Mediator (the Arbiter, Agent) is superior and more excellent, [because] it is enacted and rests upon more important (sublimer), higher, and nobler (promises) (Hebrews 8:6 AMP).

New Covenant

Christ combined His mind and heart together.

For this is the covenant that I will make with the house of Israel after those days, says the Lord: I will imprint my laws upon their minds, even upon their innermost thoughts and understanding, and engrave them upon their hearts; and I will be their God, and they shall be my people (Hebrews 8:10 AMP).

Mother Estella Boyd reminded me of Christ's sacrificial work finished in Hebrew 10:16:

This is the covenant I will make with them after those days, saith the Lord, I will put my laws into their hearts, and in their minds will I write them.

She would teach on the renewed heart in depth; here are

some of the scriptures:

> *And I will give them one heart [a new heart] and I will put a new spirit within them; and I will take the stony [unnaturally hardened] heart out of their flesh, and will give them a heart of flesh [sensitive and responsive to the touch of their God] (Ezekiel 11:19 AMP). (See also Ezekiel 18:31; Ephesians 4:22-24, 2 Corinthians 3:3).*

> *A new heart will I give you and a new spirit will I put within you, and I will take away the stony heart out of your flesh and give you a heart of flesh. And I will put my Spirit within you and cause you to walk in My statutes and you shall heed My ordinances and do them. And you shall dwell in the land that I gave to your fathers; and ye shall be My people, and I will be your God. I will also save you from all your uncleanness, and I will call forth the grain and make it abundant and lay no famine on you (Ezekiel 36:26-29 AMP).*

When you are set apart and God gives you a new heart, the Holy Spirit will regenerate you, and take away the hardness in your heart. You will understand how believers walk in God's statutes and obey them. Mother Boyd had an in depth teaching on the brand new heart. God will give you a new spirit that loves to do His will. When God would give her to lay hands on us she would lay her hand right where the heart is. When she released her hand from your chest, anything in your heart that was not like God, would be released. Many people would testify about the transformation that took place in their lives. Then, you would not mind saying to the Lord: *My heart is fixed, O God, my heart is fixed; I will sing and give praise* (Psalm 57:7).

Psalm 57 reminds me of how Mother Boyd was set

apart for God. She would tell the truth about herself and teach us to tell the truth about ourselves. You can see how successful she was in her God given ministry; she gained respect from leaders everywhere we traveled. Nothing that she would face would stop her from praising God.

When I traveled with her, we would also study in depth Jeremiah 24:7 AMP:

> *And I will give them a heart to know (recognize, understand, and be acquainted with) Me, that I am the Lord; and they will be My people, and I will be their God, for they will return to me with their whole heart.*

(This is my favorite scripture because God told me that He would give me a heart to know Him). Trusting in the living Word by giving God our whole heart is what He wants. He wants a personal relationship with us, where it is affecting every part of our life. He does not need what we have, but we need to be set apart for Him. Sanctification is the will of God.

> *But as for that [seed] in the good soil, these are [the people] who, hearing the Word, hold it fast in a just (noble, virtuous) and worthy heart, and steadily bring forth fruit with patience (Luke 8:15 AMP).*

Mother Estella Boyd told my husband and me to search out the words: SEED, NOBLE and VINE.

Seed: *Now the meaning of the parable is this: The seed is the Word of God* (Luke 8:11 AMP).

Noble: *Now these [Jews] were better disposed and more noble than those in Thessalonica, for they were entirely ready and accepted and* welcomed the message [concerning the attainment through Christ of eternal salvation in the Kingdom of God] with inclination of mind and eagerness, searching and examining the Scriptures daily to see if these things were so* (Acts 17:11 AMP). Vine: *I Am the True Vine, and My Father is the vinedresser* (John 15:1 AMP).

Jesus Christ: The Perfect Example

Jesus shows us that we need to accept His sacrifice by opening ourselves to receive the fullness of God. We must let Jesus sanctify us for Himself. We must do this by letting go of our will and accepting His will.

And going a little farther, He threw Himself upon the ground on His face and prayed saying, My Father, if it be possible, let this cup pass away from Me; nevertheless, not what I will [not what I desire], but as You will and desire (Matthew 26:39 AMP).

He went away again the second time, and prayed, saying, O my Father, if this cup may not pass away from me, except I drink it, thy will be done (Matthew 26:42).

In this scripture, Christ shows He is totally submitted to the Father. We need to be in total obedience to His will. Jesus as our example gave up His life for us; He wants to please the Father and to receive us.

I am able to do nothing from Myself [independently, of My own accord--but only as I am taught by God and as I get His orders]. Even as I hear, I judge [I decide as I am bidden to decide. As the voice comes to Me, so I give a decision], and My judgment is right (just, righteous), because I do not seek or consult My own will [I have no desire to do what is pleasing to Myself, My own aim, My own purpose] but only the will and pleasure of the Father Who sent Me (John 5:30 AMP).

Jesus always sought only the will of the Father, because the Father and the Son always act as one: In John 10:30 *I and the Father are One*, Jesus brings clarity to the two divine persons.

When people see a saint that has allowed God's will to be done, they can know that person has accepted Jesus and the work through Him.

But if I do them, even though you do not believe Me or have faith in Me, [at least] believe the works and have faith in what I do, in order that you may know and understand [clearly] that the Father is in Me, and I am in the Father [One with Him] (John 10:38 AMP).

Do you not believe that I am in the Father, and that the Father is in Me? What I am telling you I do not say on My own authority and of My own accord; but the Father Who lives continually in Me does the (His) works (His own miracles, deeds of power). Believe Me that I am in the Father and the Father in Me; or else believe Me for the sake of the [very] works themselves. [If you cannot trust Me, at least let these works that I do in My Father's name convince you] (John 14:10-11 AMP).

Mother Estella Boyd would pray for God to make us one with Him as Jesus is:

(John 17:11 AMP) And [now] I am no more in the world, but these are [still] in the world, and I am coming to You. Holy Father, keep in Your Name [in the knowledge of Yourself] those whom You have given Me, that they may be one

as We [are one].

(John 17:22 AMP) I have given to them the glory and honor which You have given Me, that they may be one [even] as We are one:

We must do the will of God wholeheartedly. It is a requirement.

Ephesians 6:6 Not with eye service, as men pleasers; but as the servants of Christ, doing the will of God from the heart;

The Apostle Paul brought out this principle to owners, slaves, employees, employers; whoever we are—we should not be people pleasers. It is alright to work while others are watching but when they are not watching, you should not slack off. When God sets you apart you are working for Him; He watches at all times.

Rendering service readily with goodwill, as to the Lord and not to men, Knowing that for whatever good anyone does, he will receive his reward from the Lord, whether he is slave or free. We work for ourselves and set apart ones also work for God (Ephesians 6:7-8 AMP).

This shows good ethics and maturity.

Now may the God of peace [Who is the author and giver of peace], Who brought again from among the dead our Lord Jesus, that great Shepherd of the sheep, by the blood [that sealed, ratified] the everlasting agreement (covenant, testament), (Hebrews 13:20-21 AMP).

Strengthen (complete, perfect) and make you what you ought to be and equip you with everything good that you may carry out His will; [while He Himself] works in you and accomplishes that which is pleasing in his sight, through Jesus Christ (the Messiah); to Whom be glory forever and ever (to the ages of the ages) Amen (so be it) (Zechariah 9:11 AMP). (See also Isaiah 55:3, 63:11; Ezekiel 37:26)

Spiritual Knowledge

John 7:17 AMP If any man desires to do His will (God's pleasure), he will know (have the needed illumination to recognize, and can tell for himself) whether the teaching is from God or whether I am speaking from Myself and of My own accord and on My own authority. You must promise to obey the word of God as you understand the Word of God. We must do whatever it says so we will not put ourselves at risk by trying to understand the Word of God without committing to obey God.

Luke 12:47-48 AMP And that servant who knew his master's will but did not get ready or act as he would wish him to act shall be beaten with many [lashes]. But he who did not know and did things worthy of a beating shall be beaten with few [lashes]. For everyone to whom much is given, of him shall much be required; and of him to whom men entrust much, they will require and demand all the more. (See also Numbers 15:29-30 AMP; Deuteronomy 25:2-3 AMP).

When you pursue sanctification you will obey and do God's will because you have counted the cost. You have realized that Jesus does not give us gifts and talents and resources merely to spend them on ourselves; He gives them to us so that we might expand his kingdom and meet the needs of others (especially fellow believers). In Luke 12, Jesus guides the way for is disciples (Notes from Maxwell Leadership Bible):

1. *Decisions:* We must know the truth and accept it.
2. *Servant hood:* We must find a need and fill it.
3. *Determination:* We must find a challenge and meet it.
4. *Sacrifice:* We must lose our life to find it.
5. *Preparation:* We must develop a plan and follow it.
6. *Action: We must discover God's will and obey it.
7. *A Gift: We must find our talent and share it.
8. *Durability: We must be tenacious and finish well.

The Way to Live

When you follow Jesus' way in integrity, conviction, problem solving, priorities, and trusting God, you will teach others how to live successfully. Here are some examples of set apart ones in Acts 21:14 AMP: *And when he would not yield to [our] persuading, we stopped [urging and imploring him], saying, The Lord's will be done!* Paul was persuaded that this was God's plan and agreed with what Jesus did in the Garden of Gethsemane: Not my will but thy will be done (see Luke 22:42 AMP). So let us keep our steadfastness for Christ is at hand. This can only be done by consecrating ourselves to God. Romans 12:1-2 AMP says:

> *I APPEAL to you therefore, brethren, and beg of you in view of [all] the mercies of God, to make a decisive dedication of your bodies [presenting all your members and faculties] as a living sacrifice, holy (devoted, consecrated) and well pleasing to God, which is your reasonable (rational, intelligent) service and spiritual worship. Do not be conformed to this world (this age), [fashioned after and adapted to its external, superficial customs], but be transformed (changed by the [entire] renewal of your mind [by its new ideals and its new attitude], so that you may prove [for yourselves] what is the good and acceptable and perfect will of God, even the*

thing which is good and acceptable and perfect [in His sight for you].

It is very important to follow the rules of everyday life. We cannot boast about tomorrow.

Come now, you who say, Today or tomorrow we will go into such and such a city and spend a year there and carry on our business and make money. Yet you do not know [the least thing] about what may happen tomorrow. What is the nature of your life? You are [really] but a wisp of vapor (a puff of smoke, a mist) that is visible for a little while and then disappears [into thin air]. You ought instead to say, If the Lord is willing, we shall live and we shall do this or that [things]. But as it is, you boast [falsely] in your presumption and your self-conceit. All such boasting is wrong. So any person who knows what is right to do but does not do it, to him it is sin (James 4:13-17 AMP).

It is important that we do not love the world. There are many deceptions of the last hour.

Do not love or cherish the world or the things that are in the world. If anyone loves the world, love for the Father is not him. For all that is in the world-the lust of the flesh [craving for the sensual gratification and the lust of the eyes [greedy longings of the mind] and the pride of life [assurance in one's own resources or in the stability of earthly things]-these do not come from the Father but from the world [itself]. And the world passes away and disappears, and with it the forbidden cravings (the passionate desires, the lust) of it; but he who does the will of God and carries out His purpose in his life abides (remains) forever. Boys (lads), it is the last time (hour, the end of this age). And as you have heard that the antichrist [he who will oppose

Christ in the guise of Christ] is coming, even now many antichrists have arisen, which confirms our belief that it is the final (the end) time. They went out from our number, but they did not [really] belong to us; for if they had been of us, they would have remained with us. But [they withdrew] that it might be plain that they all are not of us. But you have been anointed by [you hold a sacred appointment from, you have been given an unction from] the Holy One, and you all know [the Truth] or you know all things. I write to you not because you are ignorant and do not perceive and know the Truth, but because you do perceive and know it, and [know positively] that nothing false (no deception, no lie) is of the Truth. Who is [such a] liar as he who denies that Jesus is the Christ (the Messiah)? He is the antichrist (the antagonist of Christ), who [habitually] denies and refuses to acknowledge the Father and the Son. No one who [habitually] denies (disowns) the Son even has the Father. Whoever confesses (acknowledges and has) the Son has the Father also (1 John 2:15-23 AMP).

Chapter 7

Vital Prayer

Prayer defined is *a devout request or petition to a deity; the act of offering devout petitions, expression of adoration, etc. especially to God. Spiritual communion with God, awareness of his presence, as in praise, thanksgiving, confession.* Pursue sanctification by seeking God continually about everything (1 Chronicles 16:11 AMP):

> *Seek the Lord and His strength; yearn for and seek His face and to be in His presence continually! We must also confess with our lips: Take with you words and return to the Lord, Say to Him, Take away all our iniquity; accept what is good and receive us graciously; so will we render [our thanks] as bullocks [to be sacrificed] and pay the confession of our lips: (Hosea 14:2). We will give sacrificial praise to God, (Hebrews 13:15). Sanctification will cleanse our heart when we confess our sins (Psalm 32:5; 1 John 1:9). God gives peace to the Gentiles (Isaiah 57:19 AMP): Peace, peace, to him who is far off [both Jew and Gentile] and to him who is near! says the Lord; I create the fruit of his lips, and I will heal him [make his lips blossom anew with speech in thankful praise]. (See also Acts 2:39; Ephesians 2:13-18, Hebrews 13:5).*

Diligent Prayer

> *Keep on asking and it will be given you; keep on seeking*

and you will find; keep on knocking [reverently] and [the door] will be opened to you (Matthew 7:7 AMP).

We have to make sure we are knocking on God's door, because He is not tight or stingy. He doesn't keep His fist tight with His grace and goodness, make your request known to Him, and answers are promised.

There are sleeping disciples and a sleeping Church (Zion). When we are set apart for God, we will watch and pray that we enter not into temptation.

All of you must keep awake (give strict attention, be cautious and active) and watch and pray, that you may not come into temptation, The spirit indeed is willing, but the flesh is weak (Matthew 26:41 AMP).

Christ gives instruction concerning prayer. You must have a prayer life, if not you will not be able to exercise faith. God wants to develop great faith in us, so do not get weak in your prayer consistency.

Luke 18:1: Also [Jesus] told them a parable to the effect that they ought always to pray and not to turn coward (faint, lose heart, and give up. (See the Parable of the Unjust Judge, Luke 18:2-8).

We have to realize the importance of watching and praying. Pursuing sanctification warns us concerning worldliness, this is why Christ tells us to watch (Luke 21:36 AMP):

Keep awake then and watch at all times(be discreet, attentive, and ready), praying that you may have the full strength and ability and be accounted worthy to escape all these things [taken together] that will take place, and to stand in the presence of the Son of Man.

The Savior, Christ Jesus wants us to know the importance of watching events, or certain kinds of trials and tribulations so that we can pray that we escape. We must realize sorrow will turn to joy.

And when that time comes, you will ask nothing of Me [you will need to ask Me no questions]. I assure you, most solemnly I tell you, that My Father will grant you whatever you ask in My Name [as presenting all that I AM]. Up to this time you have not asked a [single] thing in My Name [as presenting all that I AM]; but now ask and keep on asking and you will receive, so that your joy (gladness, delight) may be full and complete.(John 16:23,24 AMP).

When you let God set you apart for Himself you will obey Christ and understand how He wants us to use our faith. It is great knowing the God we serve is alive, Who shall always be, Who is presented, Who is whatever we need, Who is here now, Who gives us life and breath.

Exodus 3:14 AMP: And God said to Moses, I AM WHO I AM and WHAT I AM, and I WILL BE WHAT I WILL BE; and He said, You shall say this to the Israelites: I AM has sent me to you!

Paul was effective in Athens.

Neither is He served by human hands, as though He lacked anything, for it is He Himself Who gives life and breath and all things to all [people] (Acts 17:25 AMP).

Thus says God the Lord--He Who created the heavens and stretched them forth, He Who spread abroad the earth and that which comes out of it, He Who gives breath to the people on it and spirit to those who walk in it (Isaiah 42:5 AMP).

So people of God must pray according to the will of God, Your prayers do not change what God has determined, you will find out He only accomplishes what he already foreordained. Praise the Lord!

Authority in Prayer

The Holy Spirit made it known that Christ is the servant of the Lord and my mentor Dr. Boyd was his handmaiden. We would touch and agree in prayer, binding and loosing. What God has already bound in heaven, He is waiting on His people to bind and loose first and we are backed up by Him from Heaven. In other words, God does not want to bind and loose by Himself. Mother Boyd told me prayer is work assigned by God.

Prayer is the act of declaring or proclaiming with authority. Mother Boyd wanted me to learn how to pray with authority, because the Lord had spoken of this kind of prayer in Matthew 18:18-20 AMP:

Truly I tell you, whatever you forbid and declare to be improper and unlawful on earth must be what is already forbidden in heaven, and whatever you permit and declare proper and lawful on earth must be what is already permitted in heaven. Again I tell you, if two of you on earth agree (harmonize together, make a symphony together) about whatever [anything and everything] they may ask, it will come to pass and be done for them by My Father in heaven. For whereever two or three are gathered (drawn together as My followers) in (into) My name, there I AM in the midst of them.

She said this kind of prayer moves in Heaven relying on the move on earth. She knew earth does not pray, but the earth binds and looses. When prayer is not in line with the will of God, you can see how many believers prayers are not working together with God.

(Mark 11:23-24 AMP) Truly I tell you, whoever says to this mountain, Be lifted up and thrown into the sea! and does not doubt at all in his heart but believes that what he says will take place, it will be done for him. For this reason I am telling you, whatever you ask for in prayer, believe (trust and be confident) that it is granted to you, and you will [get it].

Mother told me that God will honor our faith, move strongholds, grant spiritual desires and promised answers in prayer.

Paul was also a man of prayer and intercession for the churches he established:

Cease not to give thanks for you, making mention of you in my prayers (Ephesians 1:16).

<u>The Christian Soldier</u>: *For we are not wrestling with flesh and blood [contending only with physical opponents], but against the despotisms, against the powers, against [the master spirits who are] the world rulers of this present darkness, against the spirit forces of wickedness in the heavenly (supernatural) sphere (Ephesians 6:12 AMP).*

<u>The Soldiers' Equipment</u>: *Therefore put on God's complete armor, that you may be able to resist and stand your ground on the evil day [of danger], and having done all [the crisis demands], to*

stand [firmly in your place] (Ephesians 6:13 AMP).

Mother wanted her daughters to remember the purpose and not lose sight on why God placed Daughters of Zion on the earth and in the Church. Our goal: *We gladly accept this challenge of faith as a help to God's leaders, His church and the entire world* (Daughter of Zion Handbook). If we accept God's purpose willingly, we gain power. The Bible says, (Ephesians 6:18 AMP):

> *Pray at all times (on every occasion, in every season) in the Spirit, with all [manner of] prayer and entreaty. To that end keep alert and watch with strong purpose and perseverance, interceding in the behalf of all the saints (God's consecrated people).*

My mentor Dr. Estella Boyd lived a consecrated life and she was a Mother in Zion, who God chose and called to stand in the gap.

> *Galatians 4:19 AMP: My little children, for whom I am again suffering birth pangs until Christ is completely and permanently formed (molded) within you.*

She told me you do not live above sin, but you can live from sin. Her purpose was to see us totally transformed so we could resemble Christ. I was so grateful to have had the privilege to travel with her for seventeen years. I stayed in the same room with her, as her nurse, and experienced seeing her go in travail with pangs and groaning while sleeping. When she would wake up and attend church services, you would see transformation in many of us so Christ would be formed in us.

She knew the Holy Spirit was the only One who can

present this work in us by faith. She birthed many Daughters of Zion and Sons of Thunder and she prayed and interceded for the churches, His leaders, and the entire world, unceasing, nonstop, constant, sincere prayers for others. She did this because there are powers in the unseen world against which we are powerless except through the aid of the Holy Spirit, truth, righteousness, faith, salvation, the Word, and prayer. These are weapons that ward off and quench all the darts of the wicked and unseen enemy (See Ephesians 6:16). Mother would also give us scriptures on giving ourselves to prayer and the Word (Acts 6:4). We will continue to devote ourselves steadfastly to prayer and the ministry of the Word. She would let us know prayer is first more important than preaching, she would always say "If you have no prayer life, there can be no ministry."

Mother was separated by God and obedient to the sacrifice of prayer, suffering and self-denial, to stand in the gap. Mother Boyd said "Yes, Lord. Even if it cost me my life Lord Jesus, I will do it," (*Daughter of Zion Handbook*). As she visited churches she would impart spiritual gifts (See Romans 1:11). She knew that it was the truth of the word which sanctioned, and that alone. Gifts were available as they are today but gifts do not sanction anyone.

Prayer for the Church

Mother had a great love for the Church, pastors and ministers, especially those who feed God's Flock. She would tell me to pray these verses from Colossians 1:9-14 AMP for the pastors and ministers and the Church.

> *For this reason we also, from the day we heard of it, have not ceased to pray and make [special] request for you, [asking] that you may be filled with the full (deep and clear)*

> *knowledge of His will in all spiritual wisdom [in comprehensive insight into the ways and purposes of God] and in understanding and discernment of spiritual things--That you may walk (live and conduct yourselves) in a mannerA worthy of the Lord, fully pleasing to Him and desiring to please Him in all things, bearing fruit in every good work and steadily growing and increasing in and by the knowledge of God [with fuller, deeper, and clearer insight, acquaintance, and recognition]. [We pray] that you may be invigorated and strengthened with all power according to the might of His glory, [to exercise] every kind of endurance and patience (perseverance and forbearance) with joy. Giving thanks to the Father, Who has qualified and made us fit to share the portion which is the inheritance of the saints (God's holy people) in the Light. [The Father] has delivered and drawn us to Himself out of the control and the dominion of darkness and has transferred us into the kingdom of the Son of His love. In Whom we have our redemption through His blood,[which means] the forgiveness of our sins.*
>
> *And He saw that there was no man and wondered that there was no intercessor [no one to intervene on behalf of truth and right]; therefore His own arm brought Him victory, and His own righteousness [having the Spirit without measure] sustained Him (Isaiah 59:16 AMP).*

I would pray these verses for my son Fred and now I am teaching my granddaughters Mekari and Mariah to pray them for the family. Mother would tell the daughters that God will allow you to see the travail of your soul.

Christ is indeed our advocate in prayer as in 1 John 2:1-2 AMP:

> *MY LITTLE children, I write you these things so that you*

may not violate God's law and sin. But if anyone should sin, we have an Advocate (One Who will intercede for us) with the Father--[it is] Jesus Christ [the all] righteous [upright, just, Who conforms to the Father's will in every purpose, thought, and action]. And He [that same Jesus Himself] is the propitiation (the atoning sacrifice) for our sins, and not for ours alone but also for [the sins of] the whole world.

I really loved hearing Mother sing the song that God has a plan to redeem you.

Christian Duty

When you are set apart for God and learn how to pray according with God's will, you can make your request known to God.

Philippians 4:6 AMP: Do not fret or have any anxiety about anything, but in every circumstance and in everything, by prayer and petition (definite requests), with thanksgiving, continue to make your wants known to God.

God will help us replace worry with prayer and keep our minds on things that are edifying. Every believer should refuse to allow anything to break your routine of prayer.

Be earnest and unwearied and steadfast in your prayer [life], being [both] alert and intent in [your praying] with thanksgiving (Colossians 4:2 AMP).

Mother said Paul asked the Christians to pray for Him and she told me to pray these same scriptures for the leaders and the church today:

And at same time pray for us also, that God may open a

door to us for the Word (the Gospel), to proclaim the mystery concerning Christ (the Messiah) on account of which I am in prison; That I may proclaim it fully and make it clear [speak boldly and unfold that mystery], as is my duty. (Colossians 4:3-4 AMP).

Wake up Zion put on thy strength because we don't pray like we use to (2 Thessalonians 3:1-5). That is why we have to pray *without ceasing* (1 Thessalonians 5:17). Apostle Paul wants us to live in an attitude of prayer, while we are going on with our day. When we live with a prayer view, when we face confrontation or encounters we will be in the habit of going into prayer.

We must pray about everything and God will direct your path (See also Proverbs 3:5-6).

1 Timothy 2:8: I will therefore that men pray every where, lifting up holy hands, without wrath and doubting.

When you pray and exercise your faith, you will not doubt the word of God. You lift up hands in surrender to God. I believe God desires to use men greatly in the church, even though there are more women involved in the church.

The Life of Prayer

Prayer has been spoken of as being the very breath of spiritual life. It is the believer's spiritual contact with heaven. No spiritual life can be maintained without it. Someone has defined prayer by saying: "Prayer is the soul's sincere desire, uttered or unexpressed," (*The Foundations of Christian Doctrine*).

It is important to pray about everything. When you pray,

your prayer will identify problems. You can intercede for those in sin or sickness. By anointing with oil and praying for restoration, you can intervene by whatever means with earnest prayer.

Is any among you afflicted? Let him pray, Is any merry? Let him sing psalms. (James 5:13).

Let's look at James 5:14-18 AMP:

Is anyone among you sick? He should call in the church elders (the spiritual guides). And they should pray over him, anointing him with oil in the lord's name. And the prayer [that is] of faith will save him who is sick, and Lord will restore him; and if he has committed sins, he will be forgiven. Confess to one another therefore your faults (your slips, your false steps, your offenses, your sins) and pray [also] for one another, that you may be healed and restored [to a spiritual tone of mind and heart). The earnest (heartfelt, continued) prayer of a righteous man makes tremendous power available [dynamic in its working]. Elijah was a human being with a nature such as we have [with feelings, affections, and a constitution like ours]; and he prayed earnestly for it not to rain, and no rain fell on the earth for three years and six months, [I Kings 17:1]. And [then] he prayed again and the heavens supplied rain and the land produced its crops [as usual]. [I Kings 18:42-45].

Prayer in scripture is not an option or merely a privilege, but a command (See Luke 18:1; 1 Thessalonians 5:17; 1 Timothy 2:8; Colossians 4:2; 1 Corinthians 7:5; Ephesians 6:18). A prayerless Christian is disobedient and powerless. To neglect prayer grieves the Lord (Isaiah 43:21-22; 64:6.7).

Chapter 8

Expect to Suffer

The definition of *suffer* is *to feel pain or distress; experience loss or injury; to undergo punishment*. The Greek word for *suffer* is *pentho* (pen'-tho) means *to experience a sensation or impression usually painful*.

The problem of human suffering is that so much of the suffering seems to fall on those who least deserve it. "How could a good God make a world like this?" is often a question asked by many. The story of Jesus, the world's most righteous man and greatest sufferer is an example of God suffering with His creation. Even though we cannot always understand God's purpose for it we know that He will bring good out of it.

The major topic of First Peter is the suffering of Christ and the glory follows (1 Peter 1:11 AMP). They sought [to find out] to whom or when this was to come which the Spirit of Christ working within them was indicating when He predicted the sufferings of Christ and the glories that should follow [them]. So I believe heaven is worth suffering for, by believers and for their own future glory. We may suffer unfairly (1 Peter 2:19-23 AMP):

> *For one is regarded favorably (is approved, acceptable, and thankworthy) if, as in the sight of God, he endures the pain of unjust suffering. [After all] what kind of glory [is there*

> in it] if, when you do wrong and are punished for it, you take it patiently? But if you bear patiently with suffering [which results] when you do right and that is undeserved, it is acceptable and pleasing to God. For even to this were you called [it is inseparable from your vocation]. For Christ also suffered for you, leaving you [His personal] example, so that you should follow in His footsteps. He was guilty of no sin, neither was deceit (guile) ever found on His lips [Isaiah 53:9]. When He was reviled and insulted, He did not revile or offer insult in return; [when] He was abused and suffered, He made no threats [of vengeance]; but he trusted [Himself and everything] to Him Who judges fairly.

God does not want us to suffer, and if we are striving to be like Him, we do not want to see anyone else suffer. *Rejoice not when your enemy falls, and let not your heart be glad when he stumbles or is overthrown. Lest the Lord see it and it be evil in His eyes and displease Him, and He turn away His wrath from him [to expend it upon you, the worse offender]* (Proverbs 24:17-18). We must understand this clearly, God will not withhold any good things from those who walk upright (See Psalm 84:11).

The Blessedness of Suffering for Righteousness's Sake

> Now who is there to hurt you if you are zealous followers of that which is good? But even in case you should suffer for the sake of righteousness, [you are] blessed (happy, to be envied). Do not dread or be afraid of their threats, nor be disturbed [by their opposition]. But in your hearts set Christ apart as holy [and acknowledge Him] as Lord. Always be ready to give a logical defense to anyone who asks you to account for the hope that is in you, but do it courteously and respectfully (Isaiah 8:12-13).

[And see to it that] your conscience is entirely clear (unimpaired), so that, when you are falsely accused as evildoers, those who threaten you abusively and revile your right behavior in Christ may come to be ashamed [of slandering your good lives]. For [it is] better to suffer [unjustly for doing right, if that should be God's will, than to suffer [justly] for doing wrong (1 Peter 3:13-17).

You can read further about Christ's suffering and how it relates to ours in 1 Peter 3:18-22.

Suffering for God's Glory

When we are partake of Christ's suffering in a world that hates him, and when you are being made into a good disciple of Christ you should expect persecution (1 Peter 4:12-19 AMP):

Beloved, do not be amazed and bewildered at the fiery ordeal which is taking place to test your quality, as though something strange (unusual and alien to you and your position) were befalling you. But insofar as you are sharing Christ's sufferings, rejoice, so that when His glory [full of radiance and splendor] is revealed, you may also rejoice with triumph [exultantly]. If you are censured and suffer abuse [because you bear] the name of Christ, blessed [are you-happy, fortunate, to be envied, with life-joy, and satisfaction in God's favor and salvation, regardless of your outward condition], because the Spirit of glory, the Spirit of God, is resting upon you. On their part He is blasphemed, but on your part He is glorified. [Isaiah 11:2]. But let none of you suffer as a murderer or a thief or any sort of criminal, or as a mischief-maker (a meddler) in the affairs of others [infringing on their rights]. But if [one is ill-treated and suffers] as

> *a Christian [which he is contemptuously called], let him not be ashamed, but give glory to God that he is [deemed worthy to suffer] in this name. For the time [has arrived] for judgment to begin with the house-hold of God; and if it begins with us, what will [be] the end of those who do not respect or believe or obey the good news (the Gospel) of God? And if the righteous are barely saved, what will become of the godless and wicked? (Proverbs 11:31) Therefore, those who are ill-treated and suffer in accordance with God's will must do right and commit their souls [in charge as a deposit] to the One Who created [them] and will never fail [them].*

Jesus talks about the attitude of the world toward the disciples.

> *This is what I command you: that you love one another. If the world hates you, know that it hated Me before it hated you. If you belonged to the world, the world would treat you with affection and would love you as its own. But because you are not of the world (no longer one with it], but I have chosen (selected) you out of the world, the world hates (detests) you. Remember that I told you, A servant is not greater than his master [is not superior to him]. If they persecuted Me, they will also persecute you; if they kept My word and obeyed My teachings, they will also keep and obey yours. But they will do all this to you [inflict all this suffering on you] because of [your bearing] My name and on My account, for they do not know or understand the One Who sent Me. If I had not come and spoken to them, they would not be guilty of sin (would be blameless]; but now they have no excuse for their sin. Whoever hates Me also hates My Father (John 15:17-23 AMP).*

Mother Boyd spent quality time with me in the Word. When I would ask questions, she would help me understand how God wants us to be transformed. By pursuing sanctification, the right attitude and perspective, Mother loved to help the poor and needy and we would talk about it. She helped me to understand the blessing and woes.

The Beatitudes

> *(Luke 6:20-26 AMP) And solemnly lifting up His eyes on His disciples, He said: Blessed (happy--with life-joy and satisfaction in God's favor and salvation, apart from your outward condition--and to be envied) are you poor and lowly and afflicted (destitute of wealth, influence, position, and honor), for the kingdom of God is yours! Blessed (happy-- with life-joy and satisfaction in God's favor and salvation, apart from your outward condition--and to be envied) are you who hunger and seek with eager desire now, for you shall be filled and completely satisfied! Blessed (happy--with life-joy and satisfaction in God's favor and salvation, apart from your outward condition--and to be envied) are you who weep and sob now, for you shall laugh! Blessed (happy— with life-joy and satisfaction in God's favor and salvation, apart from your outward condition--and to be envied) are you when people despise (hate) you, and when they exclude and excommunicate you [as disreputable] and revile and denounce you and defame and cast out and spurn your name as evil (wicked) on account of the Son of Man. Rejoice and be glad at such a time and exult and leap for joy, for behold, your reward is rich and great and strong and intense and abundant in heaven; for even so their forefathers treated the prophets. But woe to (alas for) you who are rich (abounding in material resources), for you already are receiving your consolation (the solace and sense of strengthening and cheer that come from prosperity) and have taken and enjoyed your comfort in full [having nothing left to be awarded you]. Woe to (alas for) you who are full now (completely filled,*

luxuriously gorged and satiated), for you shall hunger and suffer want! Woe to (alas for) you who laugh now, for you shall mourn and weep and wail! Woe to (alas for) you when everyone speaks fairly and handsomely of you and praises you, for even so their forefathers did to the false prophets.

Accepting reproach for Jesus' name means that the spirit of glory already rest upon the believer (1 Peter 4:16 AMP).

But if [one is ill-treated and suffers] as a Christian' [which he is contemptuously called], let him not be ashamed, but give glory to God that he is [deemed worthy to suffer] in this name.

We need to accept that it is God's will for us to suffer (1 Thessalonians 3:3-4; we will glory in it in Romans 5:3). The good thing between the present suffering and coming glory is found in Romans 8:17-18 AMP:

And if we are [His] children, then we are [His] heirs also: heirs of God and fellow heirs with Christ [sharing His inheritance with Him]; only we must share His suffering if we are to share His glory. [But what of that?] For I consider that the sufferings of this present time (this present life) are not worthy being compared with the glory that is about to be revealed to us and for us and conferred on us!

Mother knew how to fight the good fight of faith, Christ reigns as King and she reigned as queen knowing that the stakes were very high. If we suffer, we shall also reign with Him (See 2 Timothy 2:12-13). When the presence of God would come in the services, I would be ready to receive the charge that God gave her. Remember present trials are only temporary, just for a season, if need be, with praise, honor and glory to come when Christ appears,

(See 1 Peter 1:6,7).

> *And after you have suffered a little while, the God of all grace [Who imparts all blessing and favor], Who has called you to His [own] eternal glory in Christ Jesus, will Himself complete and make you what you ought to be, establish and ground you securely, and strengthen, and settle you (1 Peter 5:10 AMP).*

Mother Boyd experienced supernatural comfort during trials. She taught us that we would have experiences as Daughters of Zion and Sons of Thunder, but it would enable us to comfort others because of it.

The God of All Comfort

We know when tests and trials come, God will render assistance to help us. Why? It's His character-He is the father of all mercies, and the God of all comfort.

> *2 Corinthians 1:3-7 Blessed be God, even the Father of our Lord Jesus Christ, the Father of mercies, and the God of all comfort; Who comforteth us in all our tribulation, that we may be able to comfort them which are in any trouble, by the comfort wherewith we ourselves are comforted of God. For as the sufferings of Christ abound in us, so our consolation also aboundeth by Christ. And whether we be afflicted, [Galatians 5:11] it is for your consolation and salvation, which is effectual in the enduring of the same sufferings which we also suffer: or whether we be comforted, it is for your consolation and salvation. And our hope of you is stedfast, knowing, that as ye are partakers of the sufferings, so shall ye be also of the consolation.*

Dr. Estella Boyd was a great example to me. I observed her persecution; it was bitter and painful. In adversity, she maintained an attitude of gratitude, rejoicing in the spirit and praising God. She wanted to see her daughters and sons in leadership and grow as she saw in the Early Church. When we pursue sanctification, we must expect to suffer for Christ's sake, because, we are learning to become more like him. (Romans 8:36-37). We must rejoice that we are counted worthy to suffer shame for his name (Acts 5:41-42). The Apostles were beaten and forbidden to preach, but still rejoiced in steadfastness and preached Christ.

Paul's Suffering Foretold

For I will shew him how great things he must suffer for my name's sake (Acts 9:16). The Bible gives us the summary of Paul's suffering [2 Corinthians 11:22-28]. His deepest concern and care was for the Church. It is so important to pursue sanctification; it will help you to have a mind to suffer for Christ sake. We become like him and know him in the power of his resurrection and the fellowship of his sufferings (Philippians 3:10). Mother let us know God give examples in the Bible, so we may find help and encouragement in the records of the suffering prophets, James 5:10-11 AMP:

> *[As] an example of suffering and ill-treatment together with patience, brethren, take the prophets who spoke in the name of the Lord [as His messengers]. You know how we call those blessed (happy) who were steadfast [who endured]. You have heard of the endurance of Job, and you have seen the Lord's [purpose and how He richly blessed him in the] end. inasmuch as the Lord is full of pity and compassion and tenderness and mercy. (Job 1:21-22: 42:10; Psalm 111:4)*

The prophets stood in a high and holy office but this did not exempt them from afflictions. Job had to go through some very dark, excruciating days, but never once during his trials did the Lord ever leave him. It helps to remember God's unchanging compassion and mercy when we suffer. Here are some trials that the believer may be called on to endure (see also 2 Corinthians 12:10; Philippians 1:29):

- Persecution (Matthew 5:11)
- Hatred (Matthew 10:22)
- Suffering (Acts 9:16)
- Loss of Reputation (1 Corinthians 4:10; 2 Corinthians 4:5)
- Renunciation of Worldly Treasures (Matthew 19:29)
- Loss of life (Matthew 10:39)
- Death (2 Corinthians 4:11)

Chapter 9

How to Receive Your Real Inheritance from God

*I*nheritance means *the act or fact of inheriting, that which is legally transmissible or transmitted to an heir; legacy.* We need to know the divine plan of salvation. God is not stingy when it comes to bestowing His blessings on His much-loved children. He has already given us everything in heaven, where nothing can be stolen, damaged, or kept back.

> *Blessed be the God and Father of our Lord Jesus Christ, who hath blessed us with all spiritual blessings in heavenly places in Christ: Having predestinated us unto the adoption of children by Jesus Christ to himself, according to the good pleasure of his will. (A foreordained plan 2 Timothy 1:9). To the praise of the glory of his grace, wherein he hath made us accepted in the beloved. Accepted of God and beloved son [Colossians 1:13]. In whom we have redemption through his blood, the forgiveness of sins, according to the riches of his grace (Ephesians 1:3, 5-7).*

We must shut out works and show that our salvation had its origin solely in the grace. [Romans 9:11; 11:5,6]

Paul in Ephesians 1:4 AMP reminds us of our choice position in Christ; I would like to say we are His chosen ones.

Even as [in His love] He chose us [actually picked us out for

Himself as His own] in Christ before the foundation of the world, that we should be holy (consecrated and set apart for Him) and blameless in His sight, even above reproach, before Him in love.

The saints have a spiritual heritage. It is explained in Ephesians 1:11-14:

In whom also, we have obtained an inheritance, being predestinated according to the purpose of him who worketh all things after the counsel of his own will: That we should be to the praise of his glory, who first trusted in Christ. In whom ye also trusted, after that ye heard the word of truth, the gospel of your salvation in whom also, after that ye believed, ye were sealed with that holy Spirit of promise, Which is the earnest of our inheritance until the redemption of the purchased possession, unto the praise of his glory.

The elect have a purpose with God because of their predestination with God.

For the children being not yet born, neither having done any good or evil, that the purpose of God according to election might stand, not of works, but of him that calleth; (Romans 9:11)

And if those days had not been shortened, no human being would endure and survive, but for the sake of the elect (God's chosen ones) those days will be shortened. And will not [our just] God defend and protect and avenge His elect (His chosen ones), who cry to Him day and night? Will He defer them and delay help on their behalf? (Matthew 24:22 AMP; Luke 18:7 AMP)

God's wonderful love produces security for His saints:

> *Who shall bring any charge against God's elect [when it is] God Who justifies [that is, Who puts us in right relation to Himself? Who shall come forward and accuse or impeach those whom God has chosen? Will God, Who acquits us?] (Romans 8:33 AMP)*

In these scriptures, you see self-sacrifice and strength in grace:

> *Therefore I [am ready to] persevere and stand my ground with patience and endure everything for the sake of the elect [God's chosen], so that they too may obtain [the] salvation which is in Christ Jesus, with [the reward of] eternal glory (2 Timothy 2:10 AMP).*

> *Who were chosen and foreknown by God the Father and consecrated (sanctified, made holy) by the Spirit to be obedient to Jesus Christ (the Messiah) and to be sprinkled with [His] blood: May grace (spiritual blessing) and peace be given you in increasing abundance [that spiritual peace to be realized in and through Christ, freedom from fears, agitating passions, and moral conflicts], (1 Peter 1:2 AMP).*

The Believer's Inheritance: From Servitude to Sonship

In the fullness of time God sent his divine messenger, Christ, (Ephesians 1:10). Christ's humanity is for our redemption and spiritual adoption (Philippians 2:8; Ephesians 1:5). We have the witness of the spirit (Galatians 4:6) indwelling in our hearts (1 John 3:24), that God is our Father. We, as saints, are exalted because we are the sons of God (Philippians 2:15) and spiritual heirs (Titus 3:7).

(Galatians 4:1-7 AMP) NOW WHAT I mean is that as long as the inheritor (heir) is a child and under age, he does not differ from a slave, although he is the master of all the estate; But he is under guardians and administrators or trustees until the date fixed by his father. So we [Jewish Christians] also, when we were minors, were kept like slaves under [the rules of the Hebrew ritual and subject to] the elementary teachings of a system of external observations and regulations [Ephesians 4:14]. But when the proper time had fully come, God sent His Son, born of a woman, born subject to [the regulations of] the Law, To purchase the freedom of (to ransom, to redeem, to atone for) those who were subject to the Law, that we might be adopted and have sonship conferred upon US [and be recognized as God's sons]. And because you [really] are [His] sons, God has sent the [Holy] Spirit of His Son into our hearts, crying, Abba (Father)! Father! [1 John 3:24] Therefore, you are no longer a slave (bond servant) but a son; and if a son, then [it follows that you are] an heir by the aid of God, through Christ.

Now before the faith came, we were perpetually guarded under the Law, kept in custody in preparation for faith that was destined to be revealed (unveiled, disclosed)... And if you belong to Christ [are in Him Who is Abraham's seed, then you are Abraham's offspring and [spiritual] heirs according to promise] (Galatians 3:23, 29 AMP).

The Evidence of a True Believer

We will be transformed one day from our worn-out, weak bodies and sinful ways for a new body. Due to the resurrection of Jesus, we will be free from sin and complete in the heavenly, holy presence of God.

Beloved, we are [even here and] now God's children; it is not

> *yet disclosed (made clear) what we shall be [hereafter], but we know that when He comes and is manifested, we shall [as God's children] resemble and be like Him, for we shall see Him just as He [really] is (1 John 3:2 AMP).*
>
> *For in Christ Jesus you are all sons of God through faith (Galatians 3:26 AMP).*
>
> *But to as many as did receive and welcome Him, He gave the authority (power, privilege, right) to become the children of God, that is, to those who believe in (adhere to, trust in, and rely on) His name (John 1:12 AMP; see also Isaiah 56:5).*

It is important to read Hebrews 6:1-6. The goal of the Christian is expressed fully by the Greek word *teleioteta* which is translated *perfection*. The idea being explained here is that the believer is to pursue a state of maturity, instead of going back to the initial rudiments of Christianity and basic faith. This fact is always clear in the salvation process: God offers the gift, but man must take the initiative to receive it (John 1:12; 3:16).

We must understand the gift as nothing that a person earns, but it is God's free offer of salvation. This is all true, even if the world may not think so.

> *SEE WHAT [an incredible] quality of love the Father has given (shown, bestowed on) us, that we should [be permitted to] be named and called and counted the children of God! And so we are! The reason that the world does not know (recognize, acknowledge) us is that it does not know (recognize, acknowledge) Him (1 John 3:1 AMP).*

God says so, and the Christian who believes it as a son or

daughter will say, "I'm a child of the King." Life is a period of waiting.

> *And not only the creation, but we ourselves too, who have and enjoy the firstfruits of the [Holy] Spirit [a foretaste of the blissful things to come] groan inwardly as we wait for the redemption of our bodies [from sensuality and the grave, which will reveal] our adoption (our manifestation as God's sons). Here in this world we are in disguise, we are not recognized as sons of God, but some day we shall throw off this disguise (Romans 8:23 AMP).*

> *For [the Spirit which] you have now received [is] not a spirit of slavery to put you once more in bondage to fear, but you have received the Spirit of adoption [the Spirit producing sonship] in [the bliss of] which we cry, Abba (Father)! Father! (Romans 8:15 AMP)*

"The spirit of bondage again to fear": This phrase refers to the bondage and fear of the law (Hebrews 2:15; Galatians 4:3,9). The Holy Spirit does not bring us into bondage (2 Timothy 1:7). *For God hath not given us the spirit of fear, but of power, and of love, and of a sound mind* (1 John 4:18). God's love inspires confidence.

"The Spirit of adoption, whereby we cry, Abba, Father":

> *For He foreordained us (destined us, planned in love for us) to be adopted (revealed) as His own children through Jesus Christ, in accordance with the purpose of His will [because it pleased Him and was His kind intent] (Ephesians 1:5 AMP; see also Matthew 6:9, 7:11).*

To cry is to express deep emotion. It is a loud cry.

This scripture shows our election in Christ:

> *Who were chosen and foreknown by God the Father and consecrated (sanctified, made holy) by the Spirit to be obedient to Jesus Christ (the Messiah) and to be sprinkled with [His] blood: May grace (spiritual blessing and peace be given you in increasing abundance [that spiritual peace to be realized in and through Christ, freedom from fear, agitating passions, and moral conflicts) (1 Peter 1:2 AMP).*

Adoption

Paul is the only New Testament writer to employ the word adoption. He used the term to describe the status persons receive from God when they have been redeemed by Jesus Christ (Galatians 4:3-7) In belonging to Christ, believers become Abraham's offspring and heirs with him of God's promise. Believers are chosen in Christ and predestined to this adoption by God's gracious will (Ephesians 1:3-6).

Notice the contrast: this drives out the fear sinners experience in the presence of the holy God and provides power to pray trustingly to God as our "Abba," or Daddy." The Spirit living in the believer gives confident assurance that one is accepted fully as a child into God's family (Romans 8:15-16). It also gives the believers all rights of inheritance and will join them to Jesus "the only begotten Son" (John 3:16).

Inheriting the glory of eternal life with God does not exempt the believer from escaping the suffering and persecution the world dishes out (Romans 8:17-18). The adoption process will be finalized when God restores all creation, giving His children resurrection bodies (Romans

8:23). Adoption has always been God's way of operating with His people (Hosea 11:1).

> *The Spirit itself beareth witness with our spirit, that we are the children of God (Romans 8:16).*

We must pursue sanctification and trust God that our hearing is clear. We also know that we are receiving the Gospel as believers and saints whom are sealed (Ephesians 1:13).

The word inheritance appear many times in the New Testament (Ephesians 1:14,18; Titus 3:7; Hebrew 6:17; 1 Peter 1:4). As I write this part of the book, I am so grateful for the privilege to be adopted by a Mother in Zion, who was definitely, consecrated to God, tears are flowing as I write. The late Bishop Jesse T. Stakes explained so clearly to me during the adoption that I am an heir of Mother Boyd and an heir of God. Heirs are entitled to an inheritance. This is a scripture he used during the adoption:

> *(Romans 8:17) And if children, then heirs; heirs of God, and joint-heirs with Christ; if so be we suffer with him, that we may be also glorified together.*

Heirs of God are entitled to an inheritance. Joint-heirs with Christ are entitled to the Father's inheritance. At the adoption, Mother said God told her to put the veil on me. The Bible brings out the mantle, the wisdom of the way she did it through the Holy Spirit. I believe it protected me from envy and jealousy; she told me to stay in the care of God.

A *mantle* is a *robe, cape, veil, or loose-fitting tunic worn as an outer garment.* Many of the prophets (1 Samuel 15:27; 1 Kings 19:13), women in Jerusalem (Isaiah 3:22) and Job (Job 1:20) wore them. The transference of the mantle from

Elijah to Elisha signified the passing of prophetic responsibility and God's accompanying power. These garments have been worn from at least the time of the Exodus until the present.

Veil (KJV *vail*) is a *cloth covering*. Rebecca veiled herself before meeting Isaac (Genesis 24:65). Her veil was perhaps the sign that she was a marriageable maiden. Tamar used her veil to conceal her identity from Judah (Genesis 38:14-19). Another Hebrew term renders veil at (Isaiah 3:23). Here veils are but one of the items of finery which the elite women of Jerusalem would lose in the coming siege. The same Hebrew term is rendered, "shawl" (NAS), "cloak" (NIV) and "mantle' (KJV, NRSV) at Song of Solomon 5:7. (Chris Church)

Abba

"Abba" is a Syrian term to which Paul adds the Greek term for Father, and He used Abba to describe God's adoption of believers as His children (Romans 8:15) and the change in believer's status with God that results (Galatians 4:6-7) ."Abba, Father" indicates a close relationship of children to the Father.

> *(Isaiah 56:5) Even unto them will I give in mine house and within my walls a place and a name better than of sons and daughters: I will give them an everlasting name, that shall not be cut off.*

Jesus addressed God as Abba in prayer:

> *And he said, Abba, Father, all things are possible unto thee; take away this from me: nevertheless not what I will, but what thou wilt (Mark 14:36).*

God has a foreordained plan (2 Timothy 1:9 AMP) and has predestined us for great things (Ephesians 3:11 AMP).

The Threefold Witness

For there are three that bear record in heaven, the Father, the Word, and the Holy Ghost: and these three are one (1 John 5:7).

God's love toward us is a reward and causes glory with the King (Colossians 3:4).

The Holy Spirit gives the witness to our spirits that we belong to God. It is the testimony of the Holy Spirit to the human spirit. Pay attention to the process here:

Children of God-Greek: *tekna* which means *to come to full sonship. But to as many as did receive and welcome Him, He gave the authority (power, privilege, right) to become the children of God, that is, to those who believe in (adhere to, trust in, and rely on) His name* (John 1:12 AMP).

Sons of God-Greek: *huici* means *mature sonship. To open their eyes, and to turn them from darkness to light, and from the power of Satan unto God, that they may receive forgiveness from sins, and inheritance among them which are sanctified by faith that is in me* (Acts 26:18).

The words "inheritance," "inherit," "heir," and "joint heir," are all from the same root in Greek.

Destiny

I experienced becoming an heir of God through Dr. Estella Boyd (see Galatians 3:29 AMP). She knew that I belonged to Christ when she adopted me. She gave me back to God. She prophesied to me that God has chosen me to be His Elect Lady and to search it out in the scripture (2 John 1:1). When I read this passage of scripture, I felt in my spirit, as if John had written this letter to me. I would ask God if I was one of His chosen and He answered me through prophecy given by my Apostle Richard D. Henton. He prophesied to me that God have chosen me and that God can trust me. Apostle Henton wrote a good book called *God's Chosen Children of Destiny*.

It was such a blessing when I heard Bishop Eddie L. Long's message on the Elect Lady that I ordered the video. His message confirmed so much in my life. I went to his leadership conference in Atlanta, Georgia to let him know that he was the first Pastor I ever heard preach about the Elect Lady. I also had the opportunity to share with him that it was prophesied to me that God have chosen me to be one of his Elect Ladies. I believe when I shared this with Bishop Long, it confirmed the message God gave him. Not long after that, he wrote the book, *The Elect Lady* and I ordered it for women taking my Daughter of Zion classes.

Mother Boyd also trained us how to build a prayer wall around our leaders. She knew that the Devil had assigned Jezebel (who calls herself a prophetess) (Revelation 2:20) to see that the holy preachers die or come down from their standard of holiness. Here is an example in Mark 6:17-29. Herodias was used by the enemy to oppose John the Baptist for confronting Herod because he was with his brother's wife. She hated John's stand against sin and wanted to kill, but she could not do it. The enemy then uses her daughter to seduce Herod in dance and weaken the King. He now gives her up to half the kingdom. Herodias wants John dead because she hated the holy preacher!

We need more saved Mothers, Elect Ladies and Daughters of Zion to pray for God's holy preachers. Mother also birthed me out as a Daughter of Zion. A Daughter of Zion is the wall of the church, and she is a high tower of intercession set upon the wall to pray, fast and travail. Read Psalm 62:1-8. She warns the pastors, shepherds of the flock regarding dangers (D.O.Z. Handbook) (Jeremiah 6:2-4).

Psalm 91 shows the happy state of the godly because of God who is our hiding place.

He that dwelleth in the secret place of the most High shall abide under the shadow of the Almighty. I will say of the Lord, He is my refuge and my fortress: my God; in him will I trust. Surely he shall deliver thee from the snare of the fowler, and from the noisome pestilence. He shall cover thee with his feathers, and under his wings shalt thou trust: his truth shall be thy shield and buckler. Thou shalt not be afraid for the terror by night; nor for the arrow that flieth by day; Nor for the pestilence that walketh in darkness; nor for the destruction that wasteth at noonday. A thousand shall fall at thy side, and ten thousand at thy right hand; but it shall not come nigh thee. Only with thine eyes shalt thou behold and see the reward of the wicked. Because thou hast made the Lord, which is my refuge, even the most High, thy habitation; There shall no evil befall thee, neither shall any plague come nigh thy dwelling. For he shall give his angels charge over thee, to keep thee in all thy ways. They shalt bear thee up in their hands, lest thou dash thy foot against a stone. Thou shalt tread upon the lion and adder: the young lion and the dragon shalt thou trample under feet. Because he hath set his love upon me, therefore will I deliver him: I will set him on high, because he hath known my name. He shall call upon me, and I will answer him; I will be with him in trouble; I will deliver him, and honour him. *With long life will I satisfy him, and shew him my salvation.*

I am so grateful that my mentor worshipped the Lord in spirit and in truth (John 4:24). She was burdened with the Lord's ministry to seek and to save that which was lost (Matthew 18:11). She was privileged to pass the mantle through the laying on of hands. Many people knew that before she went on to be with the Lord, her focus was never on material things. Her ambition and affection were on things above (Colossians 3:1,2). God gave her the power of spiritual knowledge of resurrection as in Philippians 3:10.

The Blessings of Adoption

The blessings of adoption are too many to mention.

> *I in them and You in Me, in order that they may become one and perfectly united, that the world may know and [definitely] recognize that You sent Me and that You have loved them [even] as You have loved Me (John 17:23 AMP).*

I like the way Jesus Christ has a course for His disciples (Luke 12:27-33). Jesus provided good instruction for His disciples on issues such as integrity, anxiety, conviction, problem solving, greed, jealousy, priorities, and trusting God. Why these topics? Because Jesus intended to guide life for His followers so that He could teach them how to live successfully.

If we were to explain the Lord's perspective on success in life, we might say that success involves (The Maxwell Leadership Bible):

Decisions: We must know the truth and accept it.

Servanthood: We must find a need and fill it.
Determination: We must face a challenge and meet it.
Sacrifice: We must lose our life to find it.
Preparation: We must develop a plan and follow it.
Action: We must discover God's will and obey it.
Gift: We must find our talent and share it.
Durability: We must be tenacious and finish well.

We have the Family name (1 John 3:1 AMP; Ephesians 3:14,15); the Family likeness (Romans 8:29 AMP), a Family service (John 14:23,24,15:8) and the Family love (John 13:35; 1 John 3:14). Jesus wants us to demonstrate love to the world. The world does not know we are his disciples, through material things, but through our love for one another, and by showing a sonly or daughterly spirit (Romans 8:15; Galatians 4:6). We will become a part of the true vine. I believe once we yield both to God's discipline and our own (Hebrews 12:5-13 AMP), we produce a life worth following. We receive fatherly chastisement and fatherly comfort.

> *As one whom his mother comforts, so will I comfort You; you shall be comforted in Jerusalem (Isaiah 66:13).*

> *Who comforts (consoles and encourages) us in every trouble (calamity and affliction), so that we may also be able to comfort (console and encourage) those who are in any kind of trouble or distress, with the comfort (consolation and encouragement) with which we ourselves are comforted (consoled and encouraged) by God (2 Corinthians 1:4 AMP).*

God gives us an inheritance (1 Peter-1:3-5; Romans 8:17).

Evidence of Sonship

- We who are adopted into God's family and are led by the spirit (Romans 8:4; Galatians 5:18)
- Have a childlike confidence in God (Galatians 4:5,6) (I will never forget when I was in prayer and God spoke to me and said that HE is my Father and I cried out to my Father and HE answered me.)
- Have liberty of access (Ephesians 3:12 AMP)
- Have love for the brethren (1 John 2:9-11, 5:1)

Dr. Estella Boyd showed love is the highest motivation for us to connect with one another, especially leaders. If you don't love people, don't try to lead them. "Spiritual leaders develop healthy relationships," Mother would tell us. We must love the Lord. We must love the truth. We must love what God called us to do. We must love people. We are obedient by faith. (1 John 5:1-3) Obedience is the test of love: love for the Church, love to God; we must keep the commandment (Revelations 14:12).

God's Inheritance

According to the Bible, believers are "heirs of God and joint heirs with Christ," (Romans 8:17 AMP) Not only do we receive forgiveness of sins, but an inheritance as well.

To open their eyes that they may turn from darkness to light and from the power of Satan unto God, so that they may thus receive forgiveness and release from their sins and a place and a portion among those who are consecrated and purified by faith in Me. (Acts 26:18 AMP; Isaiah 42:7,16)

This is in contrast with the inheritance of Israel, which the Old Testament identifies some scores of the land of Palestine (Exodus 32:13; Isaiah 60:21). The Christian's inheritance is said to be in Christ (Ephesians 1:11 AMP):

> *In Him we also were made [God's] heritage (portion) and we obtained an inheritance; for we had been foreordained (chosen and appointed beforehand) in accordance with His purpose, Who works out everything in agreement with the counsel and design of His [own] will,*

We also have an inheritance in light.

> *Giving thanks to the Father, Who has qualified and made us fit to share the portion which is the inheritance of the saints (God's holy people) in light (Colossians 1:12 AMP).*

We are made fit for it by God the Father.

> *The earnest or guarantee that we shall receive it is the Holy Spirit who, in the moment we are saved, seals us unto the day of redemption. That [Spirit] is the guarantee of our inheritance [the firstfruits, the pledge and foretaste, the down payment on our heritage], in anticipation of its full redemption and our acquiring [complete] possession of it--to the praise of His glory, (Ephesians 1:14 AMP).*

It is a true fact that believers are given their inheritance because, we are born again into the family of God. It is illustrated in brief but astonishing terms:

> *It is incorruptible, or beyond the reach of decay and ruin. It is undefiled, or beyond the reach of sin. It does not fade away, which puts it beyond the reach of time and change 1 Peter 1:3-4.*

When I would talk to Mother about material things, she informed me that it is reserved for us in heaven. It is beyond the reach of being lost or having to worry about it being stolen. She not only knew our inheritance was kept safely for us, but the Bible reveals that we who are to receive it are kept by the power of God until it becomes ours in the last time (1 Peter 1:5).

Deed of Inheritance

> *NOW FAITH is the assurance (the confirmation, the title deed) of the things [we] hope for, being the proof of things [we] do not see and the conviction of their reality [faith perceiving as real fact what is not revealed to the senses] (Hebrews 11:1 AMP).*

Substance means *the material of which anything is made or consists; matter, stuff, reality, and realness. Evidence* is *the Bible proof of a thing; the testimony, the legal material submitted, our faith is exchanged as a means of currency to receive what we need from the Word of God.*) You have to use faith to receive from God. You use money to receive from the world. God's children were led through the wilderness from Egypt to Canaan. The process of God is leaving from a life of sin to a life of pursuing sanctification to a spirit filled life. Children of God cannot jump from a life of sin into the Promised Land, we have to go through the wilderness experience first, then into the Promised Land. Read 1 Corinthians 2:9-10; 2 Peter 3:4; Colossians 3:23-24; Psalm 37:37.

Joshua and Caleb

Joshua and Caleb had another spirit, the spirit of faith.

> *But my servant Caleb, because he had another spirit with him, and hath followed me fully, him will I bring into the land whereinto he went; and his seed shall possess it (Numbers 14:20-24).*

God will not do for us what He promised to do for Caleb if we rebel. God takes full responsibility for our needs when we obey him wholeheartedly.

> *We having the same spirit of faith, according as it is written, I believed, and therefore have I spoken; we also believe, and therefore speak (2 Corinthians 4:13).*

They were wholly following the Lord (Numbers 32:11-12). Their faith took them from Egypt to the wilderness and into the Promised Land (see Joshua 14:6-15). Due to their faith, they received their inheritance and their faith pleased God (Hebrews 11:6 AMP). Caleb said we are well able to take the land (inheritance) (Numbers 13:17-32). The other spies said we are as grasshoppers in their sight and as we were in our sight so were we in their sight (Numbers 13:33). Fear and unbelief caused them to not receive their inheritance from God because they were people of no faith (Psalm 78:22-32).

> *And He said, I will hide My face from them, I will see what their end will be; for they are a perverse generation, children in whom is no faithfulness (Deuteronomy 32:20 AMP).*

The angel of the Lord spoke to Joshua in Zechariah 3:1-10. The Lord sanctified Joshua and changed his garment so that he would receive God's inheritance for him. Fearful and unbelieving people will be found in the lake of fire (Revelation 21:8 AMP).

Heirs of God

> We have salvation not by the Law, but through faith. *For the promise, that he should be the heir of the world, was not to Abraham, or to his seed, through the law, but through*

> *the righteousness of faith (Romans 4:13; Romans 8:17).*

> *And if ye be Christ's, then are ye Abraham's seed, and heirs according to the promise (Galatians 3:29).*

> *Therefore, you are no longer a slave (bond servant) but a son; and if a son, then [it follows that you are] an heir by the aid of God, through Christ (Galatians 4:7 AMP). That being justified by his grace, we should be made heirs according to the hope of eternal life. (Titus 3:7)*

> *Are they not all ministering spirits, sent forth to minister for them who shall be heirs of salvation? (Hebrews 1:14)*

> *Wherein God, willing more abundantly to shew unto the heirs of promise the immutability of his counsel, confirmed it by an oath: (Hebrews 6:17)*

We have a spiritual heritage.

> *For thou, O God, hast heard my vows: thou hast given me the heritage of those that fear thy name (Psalm 61:5).*

> *Thy testimonies have I taken as an heritage for ever: for they are the rejoicing of my heart (Psalm 119:111).*

> *And now, brethren, I commend you to God, and to the word of his grace, which is able to build you up, and to give you an inheritance among all them which are sanctified (Acts 20:32).*

Read Colossians 3:24; 1 Peter 1:4.

Wisdom

Wisdom is enduring. *Riches and honor are with me, enduring wealth and righteousness (uprightness in every area and relation, and right standing with God)* (Proverbs 8:18 AMP). Mother would anoint our hands, so we would prosper in God because she knew God's way is right. *Length of days is in her right hand, and in her left hand are riches and honor* (Proverbs 3:16 AMP, see also Proverbs 8:12-21; 1 Timothy 4:8).

Wisdom makes the difference. Mother Boyd dwelled in wisdom and she birthed the spirit of discernment in my life through the laying on hands.

And Joshua the son of Nun was full of the spirit of wisdom; for Moses had laid his hands upon him: and the children of Israel hearkened unto him, and did as the Lord commanded Moses (Deuteronomy 34:9).

Wisdom causes us to prosper God's way.

That I may cause those who love me to inherit [true] riches and that I may fill their treasures (Proverbs 8:21 AMP).

And his master saw that the Lord was with him, and that the Lord made all that he did to prosper in his had (Genesis 39:3)

Keep therefore the words of this covenant, and do them, that ye may prosper in all that ye do (Deuteronomy 29:9).

Then shalt thou prosper, if thou takest heed to fulfill the statutes and judgments which the Lord charged Moses with concerning Israel: be strong, and of good courage; dread not, nor be dismayed (1 Chronicles 22:13).

This is good advice today and still true. Obedience always bring blessing.

> *Believe in the Lord your God, so shall ye be established; believe his prophets, so shall ye prosper (2 Chronicles 20:20).*

If you want to see God's blessing in your life stake your life on His word.

> *Every word of God is pure: he is a shield unto them that put their trust in him (Proverbs 30:5).*

Mother was a true prophetess, and her words didn't fall to the ground, (1 Samuel 3:19). She told me to set my heart to seek the Lord and I obeyed and I am still obeying it (2 Chronicles 26:5). When you seek the Lord with all your heart, not with your money, you will prosper.

> *And in every work that he began in the service of the house of God, and in the law, and in the commandments, to seek his God, he did it with all his heart and prospered (2 Chronicles 31:21).*

Hezekiah prospered in all his work (2 Chronicles 32:30) and Nehemiah had confidence in God to prosper them (Nehemiah 2:20). People of God just be planted like a tree by the rivers of waters (Psalm 1:3). God loves blessing His obedient children.

First Place

God claims first place before all the possessions of men.

A. When you put God's kingdom first, you will prosper. Doing this, you will not have to worry. *But seek (aim at and strive after) first of all His Kingdom and His righteousness (His way of doing and being right), and then all these things taken together will be given you besides* (Matthew 6:33 AMP).

B. God's Blessing--*The blessing of the Lord, it maketh rich, and he addeth no sorrow with it* (Proverbs 10:22).

C. A Paradox, *One man considers himself rich, yet has nothing [to keep permanently]; another man considers himself poor, yet has great [and indestructible] riches* (Proverbs 13:7 AMP; see also Proverbs 12:9; Luke 12:13-21).

D. Discovered by Spiritual Vision--When you learn about having the blessing of God; hold fast to it by faith.

By having the eyes of your heart flooded with light, so that you can know and understand the hope to which He has called you, and how rich is His glorious inheritance in the saints (His set-apart ones) (Ephesians 1:18 AMP).

Mother Boyd taught us to pray that we will hold the riches of our inheritance hope, calling, glory and power. She wanted us to be with one spirit with Christ. She carried empowerment, influence and confidence and a strong sense of identity and she was secure in it. I remember when she received her Doctorate of Divinity from Dr. Mendez, the late Dr. Donald Henton, and Dr. Apostle R.D. Henton; Dr. Mendez asked me what are some of her weaknesses. I told him he would have to ask God because she never showed any weakness at all, she always showed strength.

E. Unsearchable--God gave Mother the task, with grace of the least, daughters, sons, preachers and the churches every where she went, with the purpose of the mystery, with humility and the unsearchable riches of Christ. To me, though I am the very least of all the saints (God's consecrated people), this grace (favor, privilege) was granted and graciously entrusted: to proclaim to the Gentiles the unending (boundless, fathomless, incalculable, and exhaustless) riches of Christ [wealth which no human being could have searched out] (Ephesians 3:8 AMP).

See Ephesians 3:7 KJV: *Whereof I was made a minister, according to the gift of the grace of God given unto me by the effectual working of his power.* Mother would always tell me to pray for God's power and I am still praying for it today. She wanted us to take this lifestyle and love it and then we can declare God is able to do exceedingly, abundantly, above all we ask or think (Ephesians 3:20). Read the whole third chapter of Ephesians, it will bless you.

F. More Precious than Earthly--*Esteeming the reproach of Christ greater riches than the treasures in Egypt: for he had respect unto the recompense of reward* (Hebrews 11:26). Mother Boyd showed the faith as Moses had and sacrificed by giving up a life outside of God's purpose to fulfill God's purpose for her life.

G. The Inheritance of God's Elect--*Listen, my beloved brethren: Has not God chosen those who are poor in the eyes of the world to be rich in faith and in their position as believers and to inherit the kingdom which He has promised to those who love Him?* (James 2:5 AMP) Those who love God, regardless of their earthly finances, position, "are rich in faith" and heirs of the kingdom. (Life Principle Bible)

I'm so grateful for my spiritual father in the Gospel, Apostle Dr. Richard D. Henton, who taught me how to love God and walk in faith and not by sight (2 Corinthians 5:7). He would teach that there is a trial of faith (1 Peter 1:7) and there is a reward of faith (Hebrews 11:6). He gave

Mother Estella Boyd to mentor me and I'm still praising God for it. He is a father in the gospel with wisdom who knows a daughter needs a mother in the spirit.

Calling

> For this very reason, adding your diligence [to the divine promises], employ every effort in exercising your faith to develop virtue (excellence, resolution, Christian energy), and in [exercising] virtue [develop] knowledge (intelligence), And in [exercising] knowledge [develop] self-control, and in [exercising] self-control [develop] steadfastness (patience, endurance), and in [exercising] steadfastness [develop] godliness (piety), And in [exercising] godliness [develop] brotherly affection, and in [exercising] brotherly affection [develop] Christian love. For as these qualities are yours and increasingly abound in you, they will keep [you] from being idle or unfruitful unto the [full personal] knowledge of our Lord Jesus Christ (the Messiah the Anointed One). For whoever lacks these qualities is blind, [spiritually] shortsighted, seeing only what is near to him, and has become oblivious [to the fact] that he was cleansed from his old sins, Because of this, brethren, be all the more solicitous and eager to make sure (to ratify, to strengthen, to make steadfast) your calling and election; for if you do this, you will never stumble or fall (2 Peter 1:5-10 AMP).

Remember your inheritance is among them who are sanctified. Pursue sanctification or the enemy will pursue you (Exodus 15:9).

Chapter 10

Called to be Blameless

*B*lameless means *innocent; guiltless, unblameable, above reproach, clear, uncorrupted, undefiled, unspotted, unblemished, good moral, upright understanding, saintly, admirable, worthy.* Greek word for *blameless*, *amemptos* (am'-emp-tos) which also means *irreproachable*.

Husbands and wives can be examples of living a blameless lifestyle. In the gospel of Luke, a priest named Zacharias and his wife Elizabeth were without children. They both walked in all the commandments of the Lord blamelessly. Zacharias was faithful to God in his duties as a priest. His wife also was faithful to God. God answered their prayers for a son after they have waited many years for as answer from the Lord. Husband and wife can both be blameless when they walk in all God has commanded them to do faithfully (see Luke 1:5-14).

Believers have to have a blameless walk. When we pursue sanctification it will help us walk in truth and behave in the newness of life.

We were buried therefore with Him by the baptism into death, so that just as Christ was raised from the dead by the glorious [power] of the Father, so we-too might [habitually] live and behave in newness of life (Romans 6:4 AMP).

We have to be dead to sin and by faith alive to God (2 Corinthians 5:7). Paul had assurance of the resurrection of the body. We remain confident that we will live again in a new and glorified body, not because we see it, but because we trust the One who gave the promise.

Walk in the Spirit

> *But I say, walk and live [habitually] in the [Holy] Spirit [responsive to and controlled and guided by the Spirit]; then you will certainly not gratify the cravings and desires of the flesh (of human nature without God) (Galatians 5:16 AMP).*

We will walk in unity and consistency in oneness.

> *I THEREFORE, the prisoner for Lord, appeal to and beg you to walk (lead a life) worthy of the [divine] calling to which you have been called [with behavior that is a credit to the summons to God's service, Living as becomes you] with complete lowliness of mind (humility) and meekness (unselfishness, gentleness, mildness), with patience, bearing with one another and making allowances because you love one another. Be eager and strive earnestly to guard and keep the harmony and oneness of [and produced by] the Spirit in the binding power of peace (Ephesians 4:1-3 AMP).*

Mother Boyd walked in love and would pray that we would walk in love also. She asked me to be her spiritual daughter when we were in the prayer room at Monument of Faith Church; she told me God showed her that I have real love.

> *And walk in love, as Christ also hath loved us, and hath given himself for us an offering and a sacrifice to God for a sweet smelling savour (Ephesians 5:2).*

> *I will accept you with your sweet savour, when I bring you out from the people, and gather you out of the countries wherein ye have been scattered; and I will be sanctified in you before the heathen (Ezekiel 20:41).*

God will bring separation; we must walk cautiously by analyzing our lifestyles.

> *Look carefully then how you walk! Live purposefully and worthily and accurately, not as the unwise and witless, but as wise (sensible, intelligent people) (Ephesians 5:15 AMP).*

> *Then we will walk in wisdom and we will have true fellowship with him and one another (1 John 1:7).*

We have to pass the test of knowing God:

> *And this is how we may discern [daily, by experience] that we are coming to know Him [to perceive, recognize, understand, and become better acquainted with Him]: if we keep (bear in mind, observe, practice) His teachings (precepts, commandments). Whoever says, I know Him [I perceive, recognize, understand, and am acquainted with Him] but fails to keep and obey His commandments (teachings) is a liar, and the Truth [of the Gospel] is not in him. But he who keeps (treasures) His Word [who bears in mind His precepts, who observes His message in its entirety], truly in him has the love of and for God been perfected (completed, reached maturity). By this we may perceive (know, recognize, and be sure) that we are in Him: Whoever says he abides in Him ought [as a personal debt] to walk and conduct himself in the same way in which He walked and conducted Himself. Beloved, I am writing you no new commandment, but an old commandment which you have had from the beginning; the old commandment is the message which you have heard*

[the doctrine of salvation through Christ]. Yet I am writing you a new commandment, which is true (is realized) in Him and in you, because the darkness (moral blindness) is clearing away and the true Light (revelation of God in Christ) is already shining. Whoever says he is in the Light and [yet] hates his brother [Christian, born-again child of God his Father] is in darkness even until now. Whoever loves his brother [believer] abides (lives) in the Light, and in It or in him there is no occasion for stumbling or cause for error or sin. But he who hates (detests, despises) his brother [in Christ] is in darkness and walking (living) in the dark; he is straying and does not perceive or know where he is going, because the darkness has blinded his eyes (1 John 2:3-11 AMP).

Walk Before God

Back in Genesis, we see the sign of the covenant. The Lord appeared unto Abram to walk before him blamelessly (Genesis 17:1 AMP):

WHEN ABRAM was ninety-nine years old, the Lord appeared to him and said, I am the Almighty God; walk and live habitually before Me and be perfect (blameless, wholehearted, complete).

Mother Boyd would always charge us to keep the charge of the Lord our God and walk in His ways. Also, she said to keep his statutes and walk before him.

NOW the days of David drew nigh that he should die; and he charged Solomon his son, saying, I go the way of all the earth; be thou strong therefore, and shew thyself a man; And keep the charge of the Lord thy God, to walk in his ways, to keep his statues, and his commandments, and his judgments, and his testimonies, as it is written in the law of Moses, that thou mayest prosper in all that thou doest, and whithersoever thou turnest thyself: That the Lord may continue his word which he spake concerning me, saying, If thy children take heed to their way, to walk before me in truth with all their heart and with all their soul, there shall not fail thee (said he) a man on the throne of Israel (1 King 2:1-4).

David's instruction to Solomon was clear and Hezekiah beseeched the Lord in 2 Kings 20:3 AMP:

I beseech You, O Lord, [earnestly] remember now how I have walked before You in faithfulness and truth and with a whole heart [entirely devoted to you] and have done what is good in Your sight. And Hezekiah wept bitterly.

David prayed for deliverance from tormentors. He also had a prayer of trust that he may walk before God.

For thou hast delivered my soul from death: wilt not thou deliver my feet from failing, that I may walk before God in the light of the living? (Psalm 56:13)

David is the author rescued from death and giving thanksgiving to God. *I will walk before the Lord in the land of the living* (Psalm 116:9). We must walk in the truth. *For thy lovingkindness is before mine eyes: and I have walked in thy truth* (Psalm 26:3). You should read the whole psalm.

Teach me Your way, O Lord, that I may walk and live in Your truth; direct and unite my heart [solely, reverently] to fear and honor your name (Psalm 86:11 AMP).

You must trust God enough to cry for help. I'm talking

about that strong cry:

> *Who in the days of his flesh, when he offered up prayers and supplications with strong crying and tears unto him that was able to save him from death, and was heard in that he feared (Hebrews 5:7).*

Mother told me to keep that love for one another as Christ commands us in 1 John 4:7 AMP:

> *Beloved, let us love one another, for love is (springs) from God; and he who loves [his fellowmen] is begotten (born) of God and is coming [progressively] to know and understand God [to perceive and recognize and get a better and clearer knowledge of Him].*

She told me to cherish truth more than anything. She told me this is especially for the Elect Lady.

> *In fact, I greatly rejoiced when (some of) the brethren from time to time arrived and spoke [so highly] of the sincerity and fidelity of your life, as indeed you do live in the Truth [the whole Gospel presents]. I have no greater joy than this, to hear that my [spiritual] children are living theirs lives in the Truth (3 John 1:3-4 AMP).*

Light Bearers

Believers who are full of unity offer a strong testimony to the unsaved world showing the God, who is love, that they preach about is real. Also, that He is working and hoping to bring others into His loving family.

> *Fill up and complete my joy by living in harmony and being of the same mind and one in purpose, having the same love,*

being in full accord and of one harmonious mind and intention (Philippians 2:2 AMP).

We all have to work out our own salvation (Philippians 2:12-15 AMP):

Therefore, my dear ones, as you have always obeyed [my suggestions], so now, not only [with the enthusiasm you would show] in my presence but much more because I am absent, work out (cultivate, carry out to the goal, and fully complete) your own salvation with reverence and awe and trembling (self-distrust, with serious caution, tenderness of conscience, watchfulness against temptation, timidly shrinking from whatever might offend God and discredit the name of Christ). Paul explains that we are to be cautious, discreet, and aware of our conduct and behavior, making sure that we exemplify, or stand for the One who saved us. That you may show yourselves to be blameless and guiltless, innocent and uncontaminated, children of God without blemish (faultless, unrebukable) in the midst of a crooked and wicked generation [spiritually perverted and perverse], among whom you are seen as bright lights (stars or beacons shining out clearly) in the [dark] world,

God's children's behavior should not be like a child who does not believe. If it does we are just as crooked and contrary as anyone else, and rather than to shine "and glow," we exit the world as dark as we found it.

Paul counts all gain as loss for Christ in Philippians 3:1,3,6-8:

FOR THE rest, my brethren, delight yourselves in the Lord and continue to rejoice that you are in Him. To keep writing to you [over and over] of the same things is not irksome to me, and it is [a precaution] for your safety. (2 Peter 1:12) For we [Christians] are the true circumcision, who worship God in spirit and by the Spirit of God and exult and glory and pride ourselves in Jesus Christ, and put no confidence or dependence [on what we are] in the flesh and on outward privileges and physical advantages and external appearances-- As to my zeal, I was a persecutor of the church, and by the Law's standard of righteousness (supposed justice, uprightness (supposed justice, uprightness, and right standing with God) I was proven to be blameless and no fault was found with me. But whatever former things I had that might have been gains to me, I have come to consider as [one combined] loss for Christ's sake. Yes, furthermore, I count everything as loss compared to the possession of the priceless privilege (the overwhelming preciousness, the surpassing worth, and supreme advantage) of knowing Christ Jesus my Lord and of progressively becoming more deeply and intimately acquainted with Him [of perceiving and recognizing and understanding Him more fully and clearly] For His sake I have lost everything and consider it all to be mere rubbish (refuse, dregs), in order that I may win (gain) Christ (the Anointed One).

Paul discerned what hindered him. He knew what he wanted: God's righteousness and not his own (Philippians 3:9-11). Paul didn't mind openly communicating his priorities as all the honors and accomplishments of his past to gain Christ. Paul wanted to know Christ, encounter His power, take part in His sufferings and finally be conformed to His death.

Reconciled in Christ

Even though we may be strong Christians/leaders, we should always state our submission to the leadership of Christ. Paul made this clear at beginning of his letter to the Colossians. He painted a picture of Christ superior over every authority on earth. Our God ransoms, liberates and transforms. Jesus is the image of the invisible God who calls into existence everything, including other Christians being leaders or authorities.

Jesus Christ takes priority among every originated thing as the "firstborn from the dead."

> *He also is the Head of [His] body, the church; seeing He is the Beginning, the Firstborn from among the dead, so that He alone in everything and in every respect might occupy the chief place [stand first and be preeminent] (Colossians 1:18 AMP).*

> *In the body of his flesh through death, to present you holy and unblameable and unreproveable in his sight: (Colossians 1:22).*

It is important to pray for the Church. We are the Church; if you take the two letters "ur" out of the word Ch__ ch, who is missing?

> *[And we] continue to pray especially and with most intense earnestness night and day that we may see you face to face and mend and make good whatever may be imperfect and lacking in your faith. Now may our God and Father Himself and our Lord Jesus Christ (the Messiah) guide our steps to you. And may the Lord make you to increase and excel and overflow in love for one another and for all people, just as we also do for you, So that He may strengthen and confirm and establish your hearts faultlessly pure and unblamable in holiness in the sight of our God and Father, at the coming of our Lord Jesus Christ (the Messiah) with all His saints (the*

holy and glorified people of God)! Amen, (so be it)! (1 Thessalonians 3:10-13 AMP)

God wants all of us to have sanctified lives when Christ returns. God will be the judge of these things at the "Rapture" of the Church.

Leadership Qualifications

A leader must walk in soberness, have good behavior, and good hospitality, when ministering and teaching of the word of God. This person must be quick to improve those areas that can damage his or her integrity.

Now a bishop (superintendent, overseer) must give no grounds for accusation but must be above reproach, the husband of one wife, circumspect and temperate and self-controlled; [he must be] sensible and well behaved and dignified and lead an orderly (disciplined) life; [he must be] hospitable [showing love for and being a friend to the believers, especially strangers, or foreigners, and be] a capable and qualified teacher (1 Timothy 3:2 AMP).

This includes Bishops, Elders, Pastors, Shepherds Presbyters and anyone else. They are all interchangeable and must be blameless as the stewards of God. They must seek to be totally consecrated to God with self-control and not compromising the word; proper.

Dr. Estella Boyd would tell me to pray for the character of leaders, not their techniques, gifts or skills. She would say what Paul considered:

1. Personal life: Blameless, not self-willed, not quick-tempered, not violent, sober minded, holy, self con-

trolled.
2. Family life: Do I love my wife as Christ loves the church?
3. Social life: Not given to wine. Am I sober, watchful and diligent, so I do not damage those who watch me?
4. Financial life: A steward of God, not greedy, not covetous. Am I allowing my leadership to be controlled by riches?
5. Professional life: (Titus 1:5-9 AMP) Titus's job was to prepare leaders.

Paul's entrusted Titus to solve problems with the leaders in the most difficult places. Mother would teach us to be diligent, because God is a rewarder of them that diligently seek Him (Hebrews 11:6). We must also be ready for Jesus' return. *Therefore be ye also ready for in such an hour as ye think not the Son of man cometh* (Matthew 24:44). We need to be also spotless, purified and blameless, (2 Peter 3:14).

The Spotless Life

Thou art all fair, my love; there is no spot in thee (Song of Solomon 4:7; see also John 14:18). My mentor birthed out Daughters of Zion to pray for the glorious church that we do not see today.

> *That He might present the church to Himself in glorious splendor, without spot or wrinkle or any such things [that she might be holy and faultless]* (Ephesians 5:27 AMP).

Mother would tell me that I must allow God to sanctify and purify me from the world when I pray. This is so that we will walk in true religion in God's sight. We must keep ourselves by pleasing God and walking in faith which will always bring proper fruit. The Holy Spirit will help us live a victorious life. *Pure religion and undefiled before God and the Father is this, To visit the fatherless and widows in their affliction, and to keep himself unspotted from the world* (James 1:27).

We have Biblical examples of righteousness. Asa's heart was loyal toward God. *But the high places were not removed. Yet Asa's heart was blameless with the Lord all his days. And did what was good and right in the eyes of the Lord*, (1 Kings 15:14 AMP; see also 2 Chronicles 14:2).

Hezekiah was also a good example. The correct prosperity can only be found in faithfully following the word of the Lord which Hezekiah did. *Now the meaning of the parable is this: The seed is the Word of God* (Luke 8:11 AMP).

And he did right in the sight of the Lord, according to all that David his father (forefather) had done (2 Chronicles 29:2 AMP).

He was full of good works Hezekiah did this throughout all Judah, and he did what was good, right, and faithful before the Lord his God. And every work that he began in the service of the house of God, in keeping with the law and the commandments to seek his God [inquiring of and yearning for Him], he did with all his heart, and he prospered (2 Chronicles 31:20-21 AMP).

Seeking the Lord with all your heart and being obedient always bring blessings. Hezekiah did pay the price to get the job done. He had what it took: commitment. The price of commitment:

- Change of lifestyle: Hezekiah couldn't live the way his father lived.

- Loneliness: Hezekiah stepped out in obedience, alone at first.
- Faith in God: Hezekiah believed that God would bless his efforts.
- Criticism: Hezekiah weathered the harsh questions of an older generation.
- Hard work and money: The king gave up the time, energy, and budget to reach his goal.
- Daily discipline: Hezekiah had to instill a daily regimen to bring about reform.
- Constant pressure: The king endured the pressure of potential failure and misunderstanding.

Job was another example. He had a blessing of repentance, being not ashamed, his boldness, spotlessness and fearlessness as seen in Job 11:13-15 AMP:

If you set your heart aright and stretch out your hands to [God], If you put sin out of your hand and far away from you and let not evil dwell in your tents; Then can you lift up your face to Him without stain [of sin, and unashamed]; yes, you shall be steadfast and secure; you shall not fear.

We all will be tested, but must stay away from all evil. We do this by uprightness, God's righteousness, and perfection as Job did.

THERE WAS a man in the land of Uz whose name was Job; and that man was blameless and upright, and one who [reverently] feared God and abstained from and shunned evil [because it was wrong] (Job 1:1 AMP).

In this passage of scripture, the word *perfect* does not mean sinless perfection, He was perfect in his efforts in doing all he could to please God, and not our own righteousness because the Bible lets us know our righteousness is as filthy rags.

> *(Isaiah 64:6 AMP) For we have all become like one who is unclean [ceremonially, like a leper], and all our righteousness (our best deeds of rightness and justice) is like filthy rags or a polluted garment; we all fade like a leaf, and our iniquities, like the wind, take us away [far from God's favor, hurrying us toward destruction] (Isaiah 64:6 AMP; see also Leviticus 13:45-46).*

We should also walk in truthfulness. Zachariah and Elizabeth walked in truthfulness, God's righteousness and His ordinances. They were blameless.

> *And they both were righteous in the sight of God, walking blamelessly in all the commandments and requirements of the Lord (Luke 1:6 AMP).*

> *What is left of Israel shall not do iniquity or speak lies, neither shall a deceitful tongue be found in their mouth, for they shall feed and lie down and none shall make them afraid. Sing, O Daughter of Zion; shout, O Israel! Rejoice, be in high spirits and glory with all your heart, O Daughter of Jerusalem [in that day] (Zephaniah 3:13-14 AMP).*

Another example was Anna, who was a devout old woman.

> *And as a widow even for eighty-four years. She did not go out from the temple enclosure, but was worshiping night and day with fasting and prayer (Luke 2:37 AMP).*

Paul strived to live the righteousness that God had credited to him through his faith in Jesus, and his conduct pleased the Lord in all things.

> *Therefore I always exercise and discipline myself [mortifying my body, deadening my carnal affections, bodily appetites, and worldly desires, endeavoring in all respects] to have a clear (unshaken, blameless) conscience, void of offense toward God and toward men (Acts 24:16 AMP).*

Sanctified Ones

Jesus' prayer for his disciples was that they may be kept. He consecrated Himself to meet their need for growth in truth and holiness. Jesus' intercessory prayers kept them from evil.

> *And so for their sake and on their behalf I sanctify (dedicate, consecrate) Myself, that they also may be sanctified (dedicated, consecrated, made holy) in the Truth (John 17:19 AMP).*

> *And now [brethren], I commit you to God [I deposit you in His charge, entrusting you to His protection and care] And I commend you to the Word of His grace [to the commands and counsels and promises of His unmerited favor]. It is able to build you up and to give you [your rightful] inheritance among all God's set-apart ones (those consecrated, purified, and transformed of soul) (Acts 20:32 AMP).*

Paul was unselfish in His service. He met with the Ephesians Elders and exhorted them. Paul was called to be an Apostle of Jesus Christ through the will of God; I would say chosen by God with a divine call. He showed the importance of how we should live. It is not enough say that we are Christians, but we must also act like Christians. Not doing so would bring dishonor upon the Name of Christ. He also stresses the all-sufficiency of Christ for the believers. In Christ we are made pure, holy and accepted by God (see 1 Corinthians 1:1,2 AMP). These scriptures bring out the purpose of God's choice and that no flesh should glory in His presence.

But it is from Him that you have your life in Christ Jesus, Whom God made our Wisdom from God, [revealed to us a knowledge of the divine plan of salvation previously hidden, manifesting itself as] our Righteousness [thus making us upright and putting us in right standing with God], and our Consecration [making us pure and holy], and our Redemption [providing our ransom from eternal penalty for sin]. So then, as it is written, Let him who boasts and proudly rejoices and glories, boast and proudly rejoice and glory in the Lord (1 Corinthians 1:30-31 AMP; see also Jeremiah 9:24).

The Sanctification of the Church

Christ led the church with sanctified ones. Sanctified ones in union with Christ have spiritual relationships with spiritual brethren.

And such some of you were [once]. But you were washed clean (purified by a complete atonement for sin and made free from the guilt of sin), and you were consecrated (set apart, hallowed), and you were justified [pronounced righteous, by trusting] in the name of the Lord Jesus Christ and in the [Holy] Spirit of our God (1 Corinthians 6:11 AMP).

That he might sanctify and cleanse it with the washing of water by the word, That he might present it to himself a glorious church, not having spot, or wrinkle, or any such thing; but that it should be holy and without blemish (Ephesians 5:26-27),

> *For both He Who sanctifies [making men holy] and those who are sanctified all have one [Father]. For this reason He is not ashamed to call them brethren; (Hebrews 2:11 AMP).*

Jesus became like us so we could be like him. We are preserved and called by God our Father (Jude 1:1). Dr. Estella Boyd told me that you cannot get what a saint gets until you let God make you a saint. God is our divine keeper. A saint's feet are ordered and guarded by God.

> *He will keep the feet of his saints, and the wicked shall be silent in darkness; for by strength shall no man prevail (1 Samuel 2:9).*

> *He maketh my feet like hinds' feet: and setteth me upon my high places (2 Samuel 22:34).*

> *He drew me up out of a horrible pit [a pit of tumult and of destruction], out of the miry clay (froth and slime), and set my feet upon a rock, steadying my steps and establishing my goings (Psalm 40:2 AMP).(This is our spiritual foundation.)*

We must be ready to do what God says to do by being set apart.

> *So whoever cleanses himself [from what is ignoble and unclean, who separates himself from contact with contaminating and corrupting influences] will [then himself] be a vessel set apart and useful for honorable and noble purposes, consecrated and profitable to the Master, fit and ready for any good work (2 Timothy 2:21 AMP).*

Saint's Portion

Mother knew her portion came from the Lord. He is the

portion of her inheritance, her prize, food, drink and her highest joy. He maintained her lot (Psalm 16:5). She knew God was the strength of her heart and she wanted Him forever. *My flesh and my heart may fail, but God is the Rock and firm Strength of my heart and my Portion forever* (Psalm 73:26 AMP). She kept God's Word in teaching her daughters and sons. We not only studied the Word, but she would have us to search the Word of God until we understood what God was saying to us. Then, we would have no reason not to obey it. *You are my portion, O Lord; I have promised to keep your words* (Psalm 119:57 AMP).

She told me let God be your refuge because God is the only one who can keep us safe *I cried to You, O Lord; I said, You are my refuge, my portion in the land of the living* (Psalm 142:5 AMP). She said "Baby, I let my soul claim God for my inheritance." Mother would teach us to keep our hope in God. *The Lord is my portion or share, says my living being (my inner self); therefore will I hope in Him and wait expectantly for Him* (Lamentations 3:24 AMP, Numbers 18:20 AMP).

Promises to the Saints

Mother knew God was not slack concerning His promises; she took him at His word. She knew that He promised to take care of His own. *I have been young and now am old, yet have I not seen the [uncompromisingly] righteous forsaken or their seed begging bread* (Psalm 37:25 AMP). She understood what Jesus says about the seed (see Luke 8:11). She knew the seed is God's message to men. Before she went on to be with the Lord, she told my husband and me to search the Word seed out in depth. Mother sowed the word in us every time we were in her presence as in Mark 4:14 AMP. *The sower soweth (continually sows the Word)*. She also told us to beware of Satan's work, he comes to immediately take away the Word that was sown in your heart (Mark 4:15).

God's seed is blessed. We just have to depart from evil and do good; God will not forsake the saints (Psalm 37:27-29). I found out when you love the Lord with all your heart, soul and mind you will hate evil.

> *O you who love the Lord, hate evil; He preserves the lives of His saints (the children of God), He delivers them out of the hand of the wicked (Psalm 97:10 AMP, Romans 8:13-17).*

She accepted the death of the righteous. *Precious in the sight of the Lord is the death of his saints* (Psalm 116:15).

Mother Boyd praised God when we studied Isaiah 52:1-12. God showed her what happens when you put on His strength.

> *Awake, awake; put on thy strength, O Zion; put on thy beautiful garments, O Jerusalem, the holy city: for henceforth there shall no more come into thee the uncircumcised and the unclean. Shake thyself from the dust; arise, and sit down, O Jerusalem: loose thyself from the bands of thy neck, O captive daughter of Zion. For thus saith the LORD, Ye have sold yourselves for nought; and ye shall be redeemed without money. For thus saith the Lord GOD, My people went down aforetime into Egypt to sojourn there; and the Assyrian oppressed them without cause. Now therefore, what have I here, saith the LORD, that my people is taken away for nought? they that rule over them make them to howl, saith the LORD; and my name continually every day is blasphemed. Therefore my people shall know my name: therefore they shall know in that day that I am he that doth speak: behold, it is I. How beautiful upon the mountains are the feet of him that bringeth good tidings, that publisheth*

> *peace; that bringeth good tidings of good, that publisheth salvation; that saith unto Zion, Thy God reigneth! Thy watchmen shall lift up the voice; with the voice together shall they sing: for they shall see eye to eye, when the LORD shall bring again Zion. Break forth into joy, sing together, ye waste places of Jerusalem: for the LORD hath comforted his people, he hath redeemed Jerusalem. The LORD hath made bare his holy arm in the eyes of all the nations; and all the ends of the earth shall see the salvation of our God. Depart ye, depart ye, go ye out from thence, touch no unclean thing; go ye out of the midst of her; be ye clean, that bear the vessels of the LORD. For ye shall not go out with haste, nor go by flight: for the LORD will go before you; and the God of Israel will be your reward.*

Mother told me that you will see the suffering servant in Isaiah 52:13-15, Romans 15:21.

Spiritual Preparation

God wants us to put on the whole armor of God. Why? So we can stand and prevail (see Ephesians 6:11-17 AMP).

> *And having shod your feet in preparation [to face the enemy with the firm-footed stability, the promptness, and the readiness produced by the good news] of the Gospel of peace (Ephesians 6:15).*

If you notice, nowhere in the Bible do you find anything about taking off the word, so it is so important that we get up every day putting on the word. Mother Boyd shared so much with her daughters and sons about allowing God to make us saints. This so we can be adorned in The Robe of Righteousness (Psalm 132:16) and the victory promised to the saints (Psalm 149:9 AMP).

A Saint in the Kingdom will receive the greatness of the kingdom under the whole heaven. It shall be given to the people: the saints of the Most High. His kingdom is an everlasting kingdom and all the dominions shall serve and obey Him (Daniel 7:21, Revelation 13:7-9). We have many promises given to us as saints.

> *Do you not know that the saints (the believers) will [one day] judge and govern the world? And if the world [itself] is to be judged and ruled by you, are you unworthy and incompetent to try [such petty matters] of the smallest courts of justice? (1 Corinthians 6:2 AMP)*

We must be sanctified to inherit the promises of God.

About the Author

In 1982, a young single woman by the name of Vanessa A. Abernathy was awakened out of her sleep three times by God calling her name. After that night, Sister Vanessa began to seek God about what He called her to do. She was a member of Monument of Faith Church and began to ask God if she was chosen. While in a service conducted by her pastor, Apostle Richard D. Henton, God gave him a word of knowledge for her. Apostle Henton said, "YES, YES, YES, you have been chosen and He can trust you."

It was not long after that Sister Vanessa was in a shut-in conducted by Mother Estella Boyd. Mother Boyd told Sister Vanessa that she has God's love and asked God if she could be Sister Vanessa's spiritual mother. In 1987, at Shalom Temple in Harrisburg, Pennsylvania, Mother Boyd adopted and christened Sister Vanessa as a Daughter of Zion. Bishop Jessie T. Stakes performed the adoption.

Since then, Sister Vanessa fell in love with God and has committed her life to serving Him. She traveled across the country serving as Mother Boyd's personal nurse until her death. Sister Vanessa has also completed in-depth Biblical studies under her pastor, Apostle Henton and continues to follow the teachings of her mentor and mother in Zion, Mother Estella Boyd.

In 1995, Sister Vanessa married her King, Victor T.

Johnson. Brother Victor later accepted his call and entered the ministry and later answered the call to pastor.

Elect Lady Vanessa Johnson is mother of one son, Fred Abernathy, daughter-in-law Monica, and two granddaughters, Mekari and Mariah.

In 1997, Apostle Henton ordained Sister Vanessa as a pastor. Victor and Vanessa Johnson are the pastors of the True Witness Deliverance Ministry on the south side of Chicago, Illinois. This is a ministry where men and woman are being saved, delivered, transformed, and discipled for Christ.

Under the covering of her husband, Pastor Victor T. Johnson "King", Elect Lady Vanessa Johnson travels anywhere there is a need, wherever God wants her, teaching men and women how to fall in love with Jesus and to experience lives that are joyful and fruitful.

Sing and rejoice, O daughter of Zion: for, lo, I come, and I will dwell in the midst of thee, saith the LORD. (Zechariah 2:10)

As a noted pastor and teacher, Elect Lady Vanessa Johnson's captivating and powerful teachings many lives have been transformed, which brought about this book.

Have you ever asked:

- What does it mean to live Holy?
- How can I know God's will for me?
- How can I go higher in the Lord?
- What is a Daughter of Zion?

ABOUT THE AUTHOR

If so, there is help. Elect Lady Vanessa Johnson is available for:

- Daughters of Zion and Sons of Thunder Classes
- Seminars
- Revivals
- Luncheons
- Shut-Ins
- Speaking Engagement
- Marriage Seminars
- Women Retreats
- And more!

Elect Lady Vanessa Johnson can be heard on The Way of Salvation Radio Broadcast Big,Gospel Xpress 1570 AM (WBGX-Chicago), Thursdays 1570 AM 9:15 PM - 9:45 PM, www.gospel1570.com.

To contact Elect Lady Vanessa Johnson, write, phone, or visit her on the web at:

True Witness Deliverance Ministries
P. O. Box 438496
Chicago, Illinois 60643
708-510-4682
electladydoz@att.net
www.truewdministries.org

References

Boyd, Estella. <u>The Daughter of Zion Handbook. 1997.</u>

Butler, Dr. Trent C.,ed. <u>Holman Bible Dictionary.</u> Holman Bible Publishers, 1991.

Conner, Kevin J. <u>The Epistle to the Romans: A Commentary.</u> City Bible Publishing, 1999.

Conner, Kevin J. <u>The Foundations of Christian Doctrine.</u> City Bible Publishing, 1980.

Evans, William. <u>The Great Doctrines of the Bible.</u> Moody Bible Institute, 1912.

---. <u>Funk & Wagnalls Standard College Dictionary.</u> Funk & Wagnalls Publishing Company Inc., 1963.

Halley, Henry H. <u>Halley's Bible Handbook, An Abbreviated Bible Commentary.</u> Halley's Bible Handbook, Inc., 1965.

Rodale, J. <u>The Synonym Finder.</u> Rodale Press, Inc., 1978.

Strong, James. <u>The New Strong's Expanded Exhaustive Concordance of the Bible, Red-Letter Edition.</u> Thomas Nelson Publishers, 2001.

Thompson, Frank C. <u>The Thompson Chain-Reference Bible, 5th Edition.</u> B.B. Kirkbride Bible Co., Inc., 1988.

Proverbs 31:10
Who can find a Virtuous Woman?
Pastor Victor found one! And we did too!

Vanessa, you are still the same beautiful person today as you were yesterday.
Your light has shined into many people's lives and now your light has come to shine into our lives.

Stay on the wall Elect Lady, so that when others see your light they will hunger and thirst after what keeps you shining, Jesus!

We Love You   - We Love You
The Shepherds

You were always special to Mother Lois and Us, since we were little girls.
Love Vivian & Deloris

Remember This Video Productions
"Where Your Event Comes to Life"
www.youtube.com/iscreamia

Fred Abernathy
Owner/Operator

Chicago, IL 60620
773-865-4422
RememberThisVideo@yahoo.com

We specialize in :

•*Weddings*• *Parties* •*Funerals*• *Graduations*• *Concerts*•
•*Stage Plays*• *Poetry Sets*• *Comedy Shows*• *Fashion Shows*•
Commercials•

When you choose Remember This Video Productions for your event, you will receive:

- Professional Friendly Staff
- Over 15 years of experience
- State of the Art Equipment
    - **-HD Cameras**
    - **-Same day DVD sales/distribution**
    - **-Live editing**
- Professional presentation for DVDs
- YouTube/ Facebook Uploads

Looking for a family Dentist?

Look no more!!!

Patricia James DDS offers gentle family dentistry for the whole family.

Receive the care of someone whose hands are led by God

That's The Tooth
2447 W. 79th Street Chicago, IL 60652
773-776-1285 ph 773-776-3171 fax

GOD BLESS YOU!!

Leak and Sons Funeral Chapels

The Founder ~ God
The Co-Founders
Rev. Andrew. R. Leak Sr. & Mrs. Dottie Leak - 1933

The Homes that Faith and Service Built

(773) 846-6567 - (708) 206-0860

7838 South Cottage Grove Avenue
Chicago, IL 60619
Three Southside Chapels Under One Roof

18400 S. Pulaski Rd.
Country Club Hills, IL 60478
Two Chapels Under One Roof

"It's Time Truth Speaks"

Visit our Broadcast each Sunday Morning from our Cottage Grove Location
9:00 a.m. to 10:00 a.m. - Over radio Station W.G.R.B. - 1390 on your dial

"Large Enough To Excel In The Field And Small Enough To Have Patience And Understanding"

Pursuing Sanctification

To Deedee

Read it

Share it — help me

promote it

Love

Elect Lady Va[n]

Joh[n]

1/12/11